Young Writers 2005 PO

PLAYGROUND

Let your creativity flow...

ode
limerick haiku
rhyme
ball...

- Expressions From
The West Midlands
Edited by Steve Twelvetree

 Young**Writers**

First published in Great Britain in 2006 by:
Young Writers
Remus House
Coltsfoot Drive
Peterborough
PE2 9JX
Telephone: 01733 890066
Website: www.youngwriters.co.uk

SB ISBN 1 84602 348 3

Foreword

Young Writers was established in 1991 and has been passionately devoted to the promotion of reading and writing in children and young adults ever since. The quest continues today. Young Writers remains as committed to the fostering of burgeoning poetic and literary talent as ever.

This year's Young Writers competition has proven as vibrant and dynamic as ever and we are delighted to present a showcase of the best poetry from across the UK. Each poem has been carefully selected from a wealth of *Playground Poets* entries before ultimately being published in this, our thirteenth primary school poetry series.

Once again, we have been supremely impressed by the overall high quality of the entries we have received. The imagination, energy and creativity which has gone into each young writer's entry made choosing the best poems a challenging and often difficult but ultimately hugely rewarding task - the general high standard of the work submitted amply vindicating this opportunity to bring their poetry to a larger appreciative audience.

We sincerely hope you are pleased with our final selection and that you will enjoy *Playground Poets - Expressions From The West Midlands* for many years to come.

Contents

Laura Mee	52
Rhys Lewis (11)	53
Danielle Higgins (9)	53
Roman Pisnyy (10)	54
Kirsty Broomhall (9)	54
Ryan Harvey (10)	55
Jessica Bayliss (8)	55
Paige Campbell (10)	56
Andrew Bilbrough (10)	56
Stephanie Peay (10)	57
Dean Sherrington (10)	57
Marie Dipple (10)	58
Reece Hales (10)	59
Benjamin Bryans (10)	59
Alex Childs (10)	60
Megan Gardner (10)	60
Jordan Rush (10)	61
Sophie Savage (10)	61
Amy Griffiths (11)	62
Laura Stonehall (10)	63
Shannon Danks (10)	64
Terri Smith (10)	64
Meghan Finn (10)	65
Jessica Pearson (10)	65
Reece Hawley (10)	66
Hannah Branch (10)	66
Reece Watters (10)	67

Ruckleigh School

Henry Mupanemunda (7)	67
Laura Newboult (10)	68
Nicholas Marshall (7)	68
Nancy Foote (11)	69
Abir Iqbal (8)	69
Lydia Bullivant (10)	70
Camani Lall (7)	70
Zoe Harding (10)	71
Isa Danyal Zaman (7)	71
Hamza Rafiq (11)	72
Grace Eyles (7)	72
Caroline Camm (8)	73

Mason Gain (7)	73
Callum Williamson (10)	74
Shyam Kotecha (10)	74
Katie Cogley (10)	75
Karina Gahir (10)	75
Katherine Hateley (9)	76
Harry Simmons (7)	76
Grace Mupanemunda (9)	77
Zoe Quinn (10)	77
Alexandra Cheung (10)	78
Katie Smith (10)	78
Muskan Shrivastava (9)	79
Samuel Maguire (10)	79
Pauline Rowsome (10)	80
Marcus Rhodes (10)	80
Edward Maclean (9)	81
Francesca Dunn (10)	81
Sam Bennett (10)	82
Andrew Dillon (10)	82
Katherine Bridges (9)	83
Elise Flaherty (11)	83
Sarah Habib (9)	84
Sophie Foxon (9)	85
Edward Evans (9)	86
Lucy Ingleston (9)	86
Marcus Powis (9)	87
Hasan Shareef (9)	87
Shreeya Kotecha (9)	88
Autumn Roberts (9)	89
Shona Williamson (9)	90
Charles Badham (9)	91
Richard Miller (9)	92
Lawrence Finch (9)	93

St Benedict Biscop Primary School, Wombourne

Samuel Russell (7)	93
Thomas Kiely (10)	94
Sam Greensill (9)	94
Emma Jones (10)	95
Charlotte Jones (7)	95
Georgina Taylor (10)	96

Joshua Rogers (7)	96
Amy Wright (11)	97
Jordan Brindley (7)	97
Zach Wright (10)	98
Christina Westwood (10)	98
Stanley Howell (10)	99
Rebecca Luter (7)	99
James Keogh (7)	99
James Randall (10)	100
Mitchell Jordan (9)	100
Isabel Lewis (10)	101
Megan Kiely (7)	101
Ellie Thompson (10)	102
Lydia Meredith (11)	103
Lucy Picken (11)	104
Oliver Steel (10)	105
Christopher Rogers (10)	106
Olivia Collier (10)	107
Emily Howe (10)	108
Ninette Moseley-Harris (10)	108
Adam Fitzgerald (10)	109
Kyle Parkes (10)	109
Nicole Stoddart (10)	109
Katie Grainger (10)	110
Kaitlin Cole (10)	111
Oliver Hill (10)	112
Liam Murphy-Parnwell (10)	113
John Howell (10)	114
Olivia Churchill (10)	115
Jazzmin Jowett (7)	115
Rebecca Roberts (7)	116
Lauren Tarrant (7)	116
Gemma Sutton (7)	116
Natasha Jones (7)	117
Lucas Chivers (7)	117
Nicholas Poulton (7)	117
Noel Howell (7)	118
Frances Hopson (7)	118
Callum Cox (7)	118
Charlotte Green (9)	119
Jack Lowe (7)	119
Jackson Mulvihill (7)	120

St Catherine of Siena RC Primary School, Birmingham

St James' CE Primary School, Handsworth

St Mary's RC Primary School, Brierley Hill

Sharmans Cross Junior School

Ryan Wilson (10)	175
Jack Stanley (8)	175
Keryn Boyle (8)	176
Lucy Barnes (8)	176
Zoë Carter (9)	177
Miriam Farrant (8)	177
Matthew Else (8)	178
Sian Last (8)	178
Abigail Bates (8)	179
Hannah Guest (9)	179
Christopher Lloyd (8)	180
Amy Canning (8)	180
Naomi Bury (8)	181
Kathryn Parker (8)	181
Madelyn Curnyn (9)	182
Joseph Stevenson (8)	182
Felicity Zakers (10)	183
Lucy Rutter (8)	183
Jack Whitehouse (11)	183
Bethany O'Malley (8)	184
Ryan Pearson (8)	184
Matt Povey (10)	185
Fraser Waddell (8)	185
Ellie Davie (11)	186
Harry Floyd (8)	186
Tom Johnston (10)	187
Remy Prince (8)	187
Eleanor Webb (10)	188
William Chadwick (10)	189
Jack Askey (10)	190
Sadie Fox (8)	190
Sean Keegan (10)	191
Toby Lawrence (8)	191
Hannah Burrows (10)	192

Springfield Primary School

Usman Ali (10)	193
Hamza Iqball (11)	193
Arisha Masood (10)	194
Salma Nazir (10)	194

Nadra Shaheen (11)	195
Keertan Kaur Loha (10)	195
Adil Abbas (10)	196
Abbas Raza (11)	196
Hasan Asmat (10)	197
Danyial Zafar (10)	197
Hasib Elahi (10)	198
Ikraam Samow (10)	199
Hibo Rashid (10)	200
Faisal Nawaz (10)	200
Mohammed Ameer (10)	201
Hafeez Aslam (10)	201
Owais Rehman (11)	202
Mohammed Hanif (10)	203
Anfal Ali (10)	204
Reece Landa (10)	205
Wasim Hussain (10)	206
Sumera Athter (10)	207
Adiba Khuram (10)	207
Aliya Yousaf (10)	208
Nisba Ali (10)	209
Abdul Azeem (10)	210
Zeeshan Hussain (11)	210
Thabat Laamache (10)	211
Masud Alam (10)	212
Sana Rehman (10)	212

Whitehall Junior School

Sanah Akram (10)	213
Sarba Khalid (10)	214
Hamzah Butt (10)	215
Roxanna Naqvi (10)	216
Tyler Price (10)	217
Lee Jones (10)	218
Sarah Arshad (10)	219
Jagdeep Mahal (10)	220
Muddasar Zaman (10)	221
Talha Nadat (10)	222
Aiysha Akbar (11)	223
Sally-Anne Cowley (10)	224

Woodfield Junior School

Woodgate Primary School

The Poems

I Want To Say Thank You For My Family

F amilies love and care for each other forever.
   Thank you for my family.
A lways running around for each other.
   Thank you for my family.
M e, my mom, my dad and my brother.
   Thank you for my family.
 I have pets called Jess, Ziggi, Bunny, Einstein and Mr Blobby.
   Thank you for my family.
L ife is cool I feel so lucky for having someone to look
                                             after me when I'm ill.
   Thank you for my family.
 I have all my abilities to read, write and see and hear.
   Thank you for my family.
E veryone should be very grateful for what they have.
   Thank you for my family.
S ome people have nothing.
   Thank you for my family.

Zoë Myatt (10)
Coppice Junior School

Thank You God For Families

F amilies are loving and caring,
A unties and uncles are kind and generous,
M others and fathers are always there for you,
 I love everyone in my family,
L ove is the most important thing in families,
 I thank God for my family and people close to me,
E veryone has problems but we all make up,
S ometimes we get angry and upset but we all stick together
                                       and stay together forever!

Katie Edwards (10)
Coppice Junior School

I Want To Say Thank You For Families

F amilies look after us and love us.
A ll of our family does something for us.
M ums and dads are always there for you.
I f we didn't have a family we would have no home or food.
L ife comes from our family.
I f we are ill they take good care of us.
E veryone needs a family.
S o we thank you for our families who do a lot for us and
help us in our lives.

Nikaela Hollick (11)
Coppice Junior School

I'd Like To Say Thank You For Your Families

F amilies are not only your family they're your friends.
A lways looking out for you.
M ums and dads, brothers and sisters.
I f you're ill they'll look after you.
L oving you just the way you are.
I love my family very much.
E ven when they have done something wrong, I'd like to say
thank you because,
S ome people don't have families anymore.

Amy Flanner (11)
Coppice Junior School

Sports

S ports days.
P roper good.
O n the field it's really fun!
R unning down the track.
T earing off the line.
S ports days are number one.

James Bracken (10)
Coppice Junior School

Pets

P ets are for life not just for Christmas.
E very day take them for a walk or run.
T ake good care of them.
S top feeding them human food, feed them animal food,

it could seriously harm their health.

Danielle Blizard (10)
Coppice Junior School

Thank God For Art

A rt allows you to let your feelings burst through your fingers

onto your page.
R edeem yourself, let your feelings be free, be glad that we
have the opportunity to perform our feelings through art.
T hank God for art.

Tom Houghton
Coppice Junior School

I Want To Say Thank You For Being Free!

F reedom is something to be thankful about
R eally treasure it because some countries are stuck in war!
E arth is meant to be a happy place to live in
E verybody should be treated equally!

Jennifer Belcher (10)
Coppice Junior School

The Endangered Dolphin

Dolphin's babies are minute,
They echo when the sun shines bright,
Their tune plays like an African flute,
And they sing through the night.

This dolphin is the prey of a great white shark,
A beautiful, calm, bottle-nosed dolphin is she
Sleeping in the ocean dark,
Her voice vibrates to another male she can see.

Endangered her species will be forever,
Lying on the coral reef seabed,
Holding onto a mermaid's purse made of leather,
And she hides in the weeds of the ocean blue as she rests
                                              her sweet head.

Emma Stevenson (9)
Fairhaven Primary School

If I Had A Past Life

If I had a past life I wonder what I'd be?
I could have been a famous Viking
I could have been a Roman king.

If I had a past life I wonder what I'd be?
I could have been an ancient teacher
I could have been an ugly creature.

If I had a past life I wonder what I'd be?
I wonder if I *did* have a past life?
Not likely!

Todd Cooper (9)
Fairhaven Primary School

The Flight Of The Unicorn

Beautiful creatures are unicorns,
With their patterned wings and their pointy horns,
They fly in the blue sapphire sky,
Their wings spread soaring so high,
I wish I could keep one.

They swoop through the clouds in graceful flight,
Their horse-like face with glare and pride,
Their flowing mane and eyelashes long,
Their horse-like whisper could be a song,
I wish I could keep one.

A swishing tail like an angel in flight,
Giving the darkness a flicker of light,
People say if you listen to the wind in the trees,
You hear the sound of hooves clumping in the breeze,
I wish I could keep one.

Rachel Darlaston (9)
Fairhaven Primary School

The Magic Rainbow

Over the rainbow,
Lives a special treat.
Slide down the rainbow
And people gather to meet.

Everybody dreams
Of their wish to come true.
The gold is big enough
To share between me and you.

Mhairi Cumming (9)
Fairhaven Primary School

The Power Of Friendship

Friends are more special than gold or jewels,
It's a treasure that will last forever,
You don't just meet someone and then forget all about them,
You remember them and never forget,
Friends are not just through childhood,
They are with you when you are an adult as well,
Through the wind and the rain, the snow and the sun,
Through the good and the bad they will always be there for you,
They will always share their things,
And stick up for you,
They are fun and helpful,
They will always play with you,
For a friend is someone special,
Who always thinks of fun things to do.

Carys Homer (9)
Fairhaven Primary School

My Gran

My gran is as thin as a daddy-long-legs.
Her hair is like a hairy colourful wig.
Her eyes are like swirling brown water.
Her face is like a wrinkly plastic bag.
When she walks she is like a superflex ruler.
When she sits she is like a lazy bones.
When she laughs she is like laughing gas.
When she sleeps she is like a snoring pig.
The best thing about my gran is that she plays with me a lot.

Lauren Ross (8)
Haslucks Green Junior School

Holding The Babies

I was sitting very still
They smelt like baby wipes
They both looked different colours
But I knew there were different types.

They looked like tiny dots
I was shivering and cold,
When I looked at the babies
I didn't know which one to hold.

I was really nervous
I heard myself say
'I don't want to do it'
So I had to run away.

William Annand (8)
Haslucks Green Junior School

The Blowing Wind

The wind is a leopard
Jumping in the air
Chewing and crunching
The food he has caught

The wind is a bird
Drifting in the sky
Lands to catch a fish
But then it passes by

The wind is a horse
Galloping in the field
The rider comes along
And they become as one.

Bekki Bowes (10)
Haslucks Green Junior School

My Gran

My gran is crazy as a monkey.
Her hair is like a horse's hair.
Her eyes are like cold eyes swirling around the place.
Her face is like a fat potato with lots of lumps.
When she walks she is like a tortoise slowly creeping along.
When she sits she is like a dog slouching.
When she laughs she is like a chimpanzee.
When she sleeps she is as quiet as a mouse.
But the best thing about my gran is she is funny
But she's the best gran in the world.

Rebecca Morgan (8)
Haslucks Green Junior School

Holding The Baby

I once held a baby called Katie Violet,
She was very cute and cuddly and sleepy in the eyes.
It was very warm and very sunny when we met,
Her fingers were the smallest I'd ever seen in my life.

Katie Violet, Katie Violet small and very warm,
Katie Violet, Katie Violet only three days old.
Katie Violet, Katie Violet scared of thunder or storm,
Katie Violet, Katie Violet the smallest baby of all.

Gabrielle Dale-Read (9)
Haslucks Green Junior School

Fluffy And Buffy

My cat Fluffy met a dog called Buffy
And together they made themselves scruffy.
They both rolled in the mud.
They met a man called Bud
And he told them to make themselves clean.

In that time they had some fun
When the man came he dropped an ice bun,
They chewed it and screwed it until there was no more
Suddenly there was an enormous knock on the door.

Abbie Field & Claire Harford (9)
Haslucks Green Junior School

My Gran

My gran is as pretty as a flower.
Her hair is like a grey mouse.
Her eyes are like crystal diamonds.
Her face is like peach and pink.
When she walks she is like a monkey doing a dance.
When she sits she is like a little duckling drinking water.
When she laughs she is like a guinea pig squeaking.
When she sleeps she is like a quiet baby.
The best thing about my gran is that she spoils me!

Olivia Steadman (8)
Haslucks Green Junior School

The Wind Is . . .

The wind is an eagle
It soars in the sky
It rides on the thermals
And rushes as in a stoop.

The wind is a lion
Roaring on the ground
Scaring the animals
And eating them one by one.

The wind is a computer
Searching the Internet in nano-seconds
The mouse is so fast
Clicking on everything.

James Ducker (10)
Haslucks Green Junior School

The Wind

The wind is an eagle.
It soars in the sky.
It rides on the thermals
And rushes like the stoop.
The winds grow faster and faster
The fastest on Earth.
It twirls the leaves like the cheetah's spots
And when it slows down it pants.

Max Deards (9)
Haslucks Green Junior School

Thunder And Lightning

The thunder is a booming drum;
Booming through my ears,
Booming over and over again;
And scaring the animals and deer.

The lightning is a flashing torch;
Switching on and off,
Every time it flashes;
It's like a rocket launch.

Charlotte Tilsley, Jessica Perry (9)
& Hannah Goldie
Haslucks Green Junior School

The Sun

The sun is a drum
Beating down
Playing a nice hot rhythm
And the light is a golden cymbal.

The sun is a mirror
Shining down a source of light
Blinding people with its reflection
Cooking people's hearts.

Katie Read & Heather Pearce (10)
Haslucks Green Junior School

Cheetah In The Wind

The wind is a cheetah
Running through the long yellow grass
All you see is black spots
Like the leaves on a winter's morning.

The wind is an eagle
It soars in the sky
It rides on the thermals
And rushes like the stoop.

Allan Whyte & Sergio Green (9)
Haslucks Green Junior School

The Wind Is An . . .

The wind is an eagle
It soars in the sky
It rides on the thermal
And rushes like the stoop.

The sun is a drum
It is round
The sun is beaming down
Cooking all the Earth.

Sam Mitton (9)
Haslucks Green Junior School

Holding The Baby

When I held my baby brother, he wriggled and jiggled,
He was so hot, I got hot as well, but I just laughed.

He looked so cute, I couldn't stop smiling
His eyelashes are long and his nose is short.

We are having a photo in the lounge
Just me and my brother on our own.

I felt so nervous in case I dropped him,
But I just held tight in case he felt frightened.

Soon he fell straight asleep
But I just thought, he's my best brother in the world!

Lucy Kite (8)
Haslucks Green Junior School

Gran Poem

My gran is as hot as a hot water bottle.
My gran's hair is as puffy as a mad steam train.
My gran is as wobbly as a jelly.
My gran is as smooth as a newborn baby.
My gran is as cheerful as a laughing hyena.
My gran's eyes are as bright as a beam of sun.
My gran moves like a snail in a race.
My gran mutters like a mumbling frog.
But the best thing about my gran is that she gives you
                    the warmest cuddles in the world!

Bethany Reid (9)
Haslucks Green Junior School

Holding The Baby

When I held my baby sister,
She was wriggly and cold.
She shook her fists at me,
She was difficult to hold.

She looked happy,
As she stared.
I felt nervous,
As Mum glared.

The photograph was taken,
On the grass outside.
The baby got colder,
Then she cried.

After the photograph,
The baby screamed.
I couldn't help it,
So I just beamed.

Aimee Wiggins (9)
Haslucks Green Junior School

Gran Poem

My gran is as cool as a master Jedi.
My gran is as funny as David Schwimmer.
My gran is as fast as a fighter jet.
My gran's hair is as curly as a clown's wig.
My gran's eyes are as bloodshot as cats' eyes.
My gran thinks she's an all time rock star.

Jake Pye (8)
Haslucks Green Junior School

Holding The Baby

I held a baby once before
It was so cute and small
I could adore it
But that's not all.

It was a girl not a boy
She played with my hair
It was all messed up like a toy.

Her name was Hannah
She had very long fingers
I bet she would be brilliant at the piano.

The photo was taken in a chair
We were both wearing pink
We looked like a pair.

When the photo was taken
She was on my lap
Then suddenly she fell fast asleep
And that was that!

Brittany Bell (8)
Haslucks Green Junior School

Gran Poem

My gran is as cuddly as a teddy bear.
My gran is as hot as fire.
My gran is as pretty as a rose.
My gran walks like she's in a race.
My gran cooks like a chef.
My gran is the *best* person ever.

Frances Durrant (8)
Haslucks Green Junior School

Inside The Tomb

Strange pictures staring at me,
Why? Why, are they looking at me?
Chests over there, stacked with gold,
Gold, gold, oh behold.
I get a fright with delight,
I guess I might drop my light.
I'm amazed, what's over there,
It's a throne, I'd better take care.
There are so many things,
Which are for kings.
I feel lost,
I wonder how much this ring costs.
Over there's a carriage with wheels,
And there's a plate for carrying meals.
There's some leopard skin, I feel scared,
I'll only touch it, if I'm dared.
We found the tomb, yes at last,
With Tutankhamun and his past.

Jessica Thorpe (11) & Charlotte Weatherstone (10)
Haslucks Green Junior School

Gran Poem

My gran is as funny as a jelly baby,
Her hair is as frothy as a bottle of milkshake,
Her eyes are like a bright sun and moon,
Her face is like a wrinkly worm,
When she walks she is like a turtle trying to run,
When she sits she is like a wobbly jelly on a plate,
When she laughs she is like a jack-in-a-box,
When she sleeps she is like a snoring cow.
The best thing about my gran is
She plays with me and makes funny rhymes up!

Katie Bond (8)
Haslucks Green Junior School

I Went Inside A Tomb

I went inside a tomb,
And inside was a golden room.
Then we saw a silver throne,
Behind me I heard a big groan.
We went up a flight of stairs,
Which were guarded by stuffed bears.
You will never guess what we saw,
A really freezing silver door.
Inside the room were golden chests,
And waiting there were fake guests.
We went back down the stairs,
And walked straight past the bears.
On the way back we saw a chariot wheel,
It looked as if it was made of steel.
That's the end of our search.

Daniel Price & John Morgan (10)
Haslucks Green Junior School

Tutankhamun's Tomb

I've opened the door,
I can see on the floor, a golden boar,
I gasp for air and stare,
There's a tap-tap-tapping behind me on the floor.
On the walls I see hieroglyphics in amazement,
There's leopard skin hanging up,
And a golden cup,
I opened the chest
And find a crest.

Matthew Stanley (10)
Haslucks Green Junior School

The Rainforest

As dangerous as a cat.
As sleepy as a bat.
As strange as a rat.
The rainforest is here.

As quiet as snow.
It's dark, not a glow.
As colourful as a rainbow.

The sound of cutting.
Let's stop this hurting.
Let's make a better world.

I'm frightened, I'm scared.
I'm gasping for air.
I'm as curious as a bear.
The rainforest is here.

As still as a house.
As quiet as a mouse.
As sneaky as a louse.
The rainforest is here.

The rainforest, the rainforest.
It's creepy, it's creepy.
The rainforest, the rainforest.
It's sleepy, it's sleepy.

Patrick Dunnion (10)
Haslucks Green Junior School

Hurricanes

Hurricanes spin like a coin.
Hurricanes are very strong.
Hurricanes are as fast as an aeroplane.
Hurricanes are extremely powerful.
Hurricanes are continuous boomers.
Hurricanes have a source of cold and hot air.
Hurricanes are an accident waiting to happen!

Jack Scranage (9)
Haslucks Green Junior School

Howard Carter

He was gasping for air,
And shaking and scared,
Deep down inside,
It was like a roller coaster ride,
Far down the stairs,
Everybody cares,
He was all alone,
When he found the throne,
And behind a huge chest,
Is where Tutankhamun rests,
The time was ticking,
The candle was flickering,
Many chests were filled with gold,
But you'd never know that they were old,
Carter was so hot,
When he found a huge pot,
Let's hope I find some,
In the future to come.

Sophie Holds (10) & Betsy Croft (11)
Haslucks Green Junior School

Gran

My gran sits like the queen,
My gran walks like a tortoise,
Her voice is like a squeaky mouse,
She often says, 'Oh love,'
Her body is a hill,
Her back is a stegosaurus,
Her face is a Buddha,
Her eyes glimmer like crystals,
Her mouth is a fish's mouth with false teeth,
She always gives me spicy kisses, *yuck!*
But when I think of her all I can see is love!

Victoria Higgins (9)
Haslucks Green Junior School

I Went Inside A Tomb

I went inside a tomb,
And inside was a golden room.
We then saw a silver throne,
Behind me I heard a big groan.
We went up a flight of stairs,
Which were guarded by bears.
And you will never guess what we saw,
But a really freezing silver door.
And inside were golden chests,
And waiting there were fake guests.
We went back down the stairs,
And walked straight past the bears.
On the way we saw a chariot wheel,
It looked as if it was made of steel.
And that's the end of our quest.

Luke Smith (10)
Haslucks Green Junior School

Gran

My gran sits in a heap
She walks like a tortoise
Her voice is a croaking frog
She often says, 'Where is my cup of tea?'
Her body is a bat, with open wings
Her back is a broken stick
Her face is like Darth Vader
Her eyes are crystal-blue water
Her mouth is a portal to another dimension
She always kisses on the lips
When I think of her I think of a wonky ninja.

Jake Lilley (9)
Haslucks Green Junior School

The Finding Of Tutankhamun's Tomb

Howard Carter found an Egyptian pharaoh's tomb,
He had searched for five years,
When he found a door leading to a room,
Inside he found loads of silver and gold,
And some other valuables that were really old.
We were right there with him and we were gasping for air,
We were happy and also scared.
There were quite a few chests filled with different treasures,
And some Egyptian sandals made out of leather.
We went further and further inside,
It felt like we were on a roller coaster ride.
We found Tutankhamun's tomb,
And his two stillborn daughters.
We thought all the treasure would be split up into quarters,
But it wasn't.
It was so quiet we could hear people's hearts thumping,
It was so exciting we started jumping,
And that is the poem of when we found Tutankhamun's tomb.

Rebecca Money & Imaan Iqbal (10)
Haslucks Green Junior School

Inside The Tomb

I opened the door,
I see on the floor a golden boar,
I gasp for air and stare,
I hear a tap-tap-tapping of a stave on the floor,
I see items fit for a king,
Red, yellow, gold and silver,
All items fit for a great king,
Like Tutankhamun
Priceless jewels, marvellous pots and pans,
Over there I see a bronze chair,
And over there I see a gold pear,
I hear a light breeze.

James Envine (11)
Haslucks Green Junior School

The Bermuda Triangle

The Bermuda Triangle is the Devil's trap,
Which ensnares boats and planes,
The Bermuda Triangle is full of fear,
And nobody, but nobody dares to go near.
Some people think it's aliens,
And others think it's monsters,
My thoughts I'll share with you,
You'll wish you never knew.
If I ever went in it, I'd be really scared,
My stomach would churn and my vision would blur,
If anything goes over the Devil's trap,
They are in for a very big nap!
The Devil's trap will always be there,
For if you go near, you're in for a scare.
Be sucked to the ocean deep,
Zoomed to oblivion in a leap.
The Bermuda Triangle is the worst place ever,
People want it to go away forever,
And every time, people say,
'Never go near and stay away!'

Bradley Damms & Mohammed Khezar Bhatti (10)
Haslucks Green Junior School

Sea Of Wonder

Sea of wonder creeps behind the sky splashing and sploshing about
The sea can never be destroyed by man or by the storm.

The sea is heavy, slow and lurching
That may never been seen or heard
Because it is the sea of wonder
And wonders it will perform.

When it is calm it is patient
When it is rough it is angry
And that is the sea of wonder.

Hiral Ladwa (9)
Haslucks Green Junior School

Tracy Beaker Strikes Again

Tracy lives in the dumping ground
Where all the kids are lost and found,
Her evil enemy is Justine
Because she is always being mean,
All the kids are weird and crazy,
Sometimes they are really lazy,
They fight and scream with Justine,
They always eat ice cream,
Tracy Beaker is always bossy,
Half the time she is always crossy
She moans and groans to her social worker
Elaine the pain that's what they call her.
And everyone thinks she is insane!
Tracy has a foster mom, called Cam,
Who has a boyfriend called Sam,
They took her out to a fair,
All she did was spit and swear!
Look how naughty Tracy is
To do such a thing like this,
Shhh . . . don't tell anyone about this,
It's a secret!

Jessica Newbury & Katie Adams (10)
Haslucks Green Junior School

My Pet

My pet is cute and furry
My pet's eyelashes are very curly
It licks itself over and over
My pet is like a lucky four-leaf clover.

My pet is very small
And keeps running into the wall
She's got a friend
Who lives round the corner and often falls over.

Amy Charles (9)
Haslucks Green Junior School

Rainforest Trees

R ainforests are never dry,
A nd most of the trees grow very high.
I n the forest lots of plants grow,
N ever has any snow.
F or the forest there is lots of sun,
O ver there few humans come.
R unning on the slippery ground,
E very little squelchy sound.
S omething jumping on the trees,
T hey look like giant fleas!

T rees are tall,
R obins are small.
E verything breathes,
E verything sees,
S o the rainforest is alive!

Ajay Mistry & Prashant Mulu (10)
Haslucks Green Junior School

The Weather

I hate the snow, it's slushy and cold.
I love the sun, it's warm and fun.
I like autumn, kicking leaves high in the sky.
My favourite weather is warm and sunny
Holiday time of the year.
Time to swim, time to play,
Time to have fun, fun, fun.
Then all of a sudden down it comes
Drip-drop, drip-drop.
Out come the brollies,
Rainbow follows,
Lovely sky, oh my, oh my.
Now back to snow
And off we go,
On our sleighs,
Great winter days!

Sheridan Jones (10)
Haslucks Green Junior School

Football Crazy Mania

F ootball's great, nobody's late,
O ffside rule is a bit of a fool,
O ff the pitch everyone's a mate,
T he tackles are mean,
B ut the players don't run out of steam,
A ll the goalkeepers are good,
L ehman is good as he should be,
L ehman should be in Germany.

C oaches are fantastic,
R eferees are rubbish,
A lways giving free kicks,
Z idane is brilliant,
Y akubu scores a goal.

M ike Taylor for Birmingham City,
A lways saving great shots,
N ewcastle United with Michael Owen,
 I n the top ten of the Premiership
A nd Birmingham City
    Hopefully first!

Sam Clark & Jonathan Phillips (10)
Haslucks Green Junior School

The Wind

The wind is an eagle
It soars in the sky
It rides on the thermals
And rushes like the stoop.

The wind is a horse galloping across the field
The grass flowing like a horse's mane
The rider on the horse bumping up and down
As the horse runs through the town.

Melissa Albutt (9)
Haslucks Green Junior School

Best Friends

Best friends always play,
Best friends always say,
'All for one and one for all,'
Best friends always call,
Best friends never fight,
Best friends always are polite,
Best friends never part,
Best friends always laugh,
Best friends always stick together,
Best friends forever and ever!

Worst friends
Worst friends never play,
Worst friends never say,
'All for one and one for all,'
Worst friends never call,
Worst friends always fight,
Worst friends are never polite,
Worst friends always part,
Worst friends never laugh,
Worst friends never stick together,
Worst friends never, never!

Elisha Bharaj & Charlotte Thompson (10)
Haslucks Green Junior School

Waves

(Based on 'Seaweed' by D H Lawrence)

Waves crash and crash and crumble some more,
As if they are running and fall
But if they crash into some fierce coral,
They frantically surround it all, bubbly and white.

Olivia Newcombe (10)
Hollyfast Primary School

Dolphins

(Based on 'Seaweed' by D H Lawrence)

Dolphins are squealing and squeaking and splashing
As if dancing in the gloomy wind,
Dolphins are leaping beautifully in and out,
As the tide bellows to the sand.

Alex Muir (10)
Hollyfast Primary School

Sand

(Based on 'Seaweed' by D H Lawrence)

Sand swoops and swoops and scatters,
As if spinning their arms round in the air,
And if they charge into a fierce rock,
They struggle to move but never hurt themselves.

Bethany Cope (10)
Hollyfast Primary School

Crabs

(Based on 'Seaweed' by D H Lawrence)

Crabs snipping and snapping and snarling,
As if they were dancing around.
And if they surround a fish
They will never get hurt.

Tom Moreton (10)
Hollyfast Primary School

Crabs

(Based on 'Seaweed' by D H Lawrence)

Crabs snip and snip and snap,
As if a swordfight, swords crashing together
And if they get seen,
They bury themselves as fast as lightning can go
They surround their prey with their deadly claws,
Always ready for action.

Ashley Hunter (10)
Hollyfast Primary School

Tsunami

(Based on 'Seaweed' by D H Lawrence)

Tsunami trashes and tanters and towers.
As if Evil is trying to cause a riot by showing off his deadly powers
And, if he crashes into a wall,
He will wash-out the land and hurt anyone but himself,
He leaves only silence.

Sophie Brown (10)
Hollyfast Primary School

Dolphins

(Based on 'Seaweed' by D H Lawrence)

Dolphins splosh and splosh and splash,
As if they were crashing in and out of the waves
And if they lose one of their friends,
They jump high and low ducking in and out of the water,
                                    lonely and upset.

Nakita Rabidas (11)
Hollyfast Primary School

Dolphins

(Based on 'Seaweed' by D H Lawrence)

Dolphins call and call and creak
As if talking to their dolphin friends
And when they get to fly over a wave
They are like a gymnast leaping over a vault.
Although they leap and fly they will never get hurt.

Emma Fitzsimons (10)
Hollyfast Primary School

Dolphins

(Based on 'Seaweed' by D H Lawrence)

Dolphins splash and splash and splosh
As if calling its crowd of friends
And they leap and crash into the waves,
They play all day and night not knowing when to stop.

Paramjit Sehmi (10)
Hollyfast Primary School

Whales

(Based on 'Seaweed' by D H Lawrence)

Whales crash and crush and bash,
As if they're like a mighty bulldozer,
And if they crumble into a bulky iceberg
They recover from it easily without injuring themselves.

Hashem Almajdub (11)
Hollyfast Primary School

Dolphins
(Based on 'Seaweed' by D H Lawrence)

Dolphins squeak and squeak and splash,
As if calling to their family and friends
And when they jump and hop into the foaming waves
They will never hurt themselves.

Hannah Muir (10)
Hollyfast Primary School

Tsunami
(Based on 'Seaweed' by D H Lawrence)

Tsunamis thrash and thrash and tackle,
As if an army is trampling down the beach
And if it crashes into a fierce boulder,
It attacks it and washes it away.

Aaron Smith (10)
Hollyfast Primary School

Starfish
(Based on 'Seaweed' by D H Lawrence)

Starfish swim and sway and swish,
As they hoover up tiny fish.
They're cute creatures that will fit in a jar,
Their appearance is pretty, twinkling like a star.

Christian Jordan (10)
Hollyfast Primary School

Dolphins In The Sea

(Based on 'Seaweed' by D H Lawrence)

Dolphins squeak and squawk and splash,
As if excitedly playing tag in the gloomy sea,
And if they dive too deep down,
They quickly swim to the surface for a breath of fresh air.

Nicolas McKissock (11)
Hollyfast Primary School

Cry In The Night

It might have been . . .
A mad scientist blowing up the lab,
Brian's Nissan Skyline revving its engine,
A policeman speeding after a robber in an alleyway,
Next-door's letter box rattling every minute,
A boy racer doing donuts on the freeway,
Or . . .
An Eddie Stobart unloading onto the loading bay,
Or a ravenous robber eating kebab meat and chips
Maybe thunder crashing in the distance,
A big wolf eating Mr Blobby's dinner,
But I know . . .

Aaron Sanders (10)
Little London JMI School

The Witches' Cauldron

Bubble, bubble
Crawl and huddle
Let's taste the awful trouble

Eye of slimy newt
A stripy yellow boot
Cry of fox
Lots of rocks.

Bubble, bubble
Crawl and huddle
Let's taste the awful trouble.

Quietly the cauldron splashes
Into merrily ashes
Tear of an old owl
And lots of grudging howls.

Bubble, bubble
Crawl and huddle
Let's taste the awful trouble.

An old man's silky hair
A mouldy, rotten pear
A grizzly little bear.

Bubble, bubble
Crawl and huddle
Let's taste the awful trouble.

Sabrina Heer   (10)
Little London JMI School

Cry In The Night

It might have been . . .
A piece of paper flapping as it's blown by strong wind
Dad's car alarm going off in the mud lane,
My sister sharpening her pencil ready to do her homework
My insomniac mom hanging out school uniform to dry,
Or . . .
My hungry cat pouring her own tea,
The old fogies dancing to Gareth Gates on the rooftop,
A dragon sneezing gooey snot bubbles in the attic,
My friends playing hide-and-seek in the dark.
But . . .
I thought that it was just a bird cheeping,
But it's still a mystery, I'll find out in the morning
But for now, *goodnight!*

Bethany Ball (10)
Little London JMI School

Cry In The Night

It might have been . . .
A dog barking loudly on the street,
A brand new iron coming to life,
A giant ant raiding our fully stocked fridge,
Mrs McKay transforming quickly into an alien *(again!)*
Or . . .
A monster snoring beneath my bed,
A hamster playing and singing, 'Queen rock!'
A helicopter and aeroplane wrestling in the sky,
A vampire sucking my neighbour's blood!
But . . .
It's probably just the train station up the road.

Harvinder Dullat (10)
Little London JMI School

Cry In The Night

It might have been . . .
Rats having a party in the dustbin,
Tracy Beaker storming at Jenny,
A couple kissing in the park,
Anastasia left outside alone,
Or . . .
My brother brainwashed on the computer,
A smelly fox being chased by a mouse,
A fierce lion being chased by Mary and her little lamb,
The mental lady going *(whoo whoo, whoo!)*
But . . .
The voice disappeared, *zzzzz*.

Navjot Kaur (10)
Little London JMI School

Cry In The Night

It might have been . . .
A wolf playing on the game downstairs,
A dog walking on two legs coming to bed,
Two rabbits in a wrestling ring at the bottom of the stairs,
A man coming to sing to me,
Or . . .
A big mouse killing a cat for dinner,
My nan learning karate downstairs,
But it went, so I went back to sleep.

Grant Carter (11)
Little London JMI School

A Cry In The Night

It might have been . . .
A cat miaowing at a policeman in the street,
A fox munching up a rabbit
A ravenous robber eating kebab and chips,
A dragon sharpening his nails on the corner of the house,
Or . . .
The thunder crashing in the distance,
Mrs Cooper slurping beer in the zoo with a monkey,
A car crashing into the house next door,
My mom having a bath in the pond.
But . . .
Tell me what it really is.

Shane Matthews (10)
Little London JMI School

Cry In The Night

It might have been . . .
A police car speeding through Aston Road,
Maybe condensation dripping from the ceiling,
Mrs Gordon chilling with a gorilla on a bench,
A drunken man talking to himself in the street,
Or . . .
It could have been the school clock tower clicking,
A burglar climbing on the rooftop after jewels,
It could have been a monster screeching in the attic,
Even a Hawaiian lady playing on the drums on the landing,
But the sound has departed, so I can go to sleep.

Jack Haynes (10)
Little London JMI School

The Witches' Cauldron

Double, double cauldron bubble,
Let us make awful trouble.
The fin of a great white shark,
Make it work brightly in the dark.
Double, double cauldron bubble,
Let us make awful trouble.
Eye of a day-sleeping bat,
Squeak of a rat, wing of bat.
Double, double cauldron bubble,
Let us make awful trouble.
Finger of a baby,
Related to a tall lady.
Double, double cauldron bubble,
Let us make awful trouble.

Samantha Longden (10)
Little London JMI School

Cry In The Night

It might have been . . .
A motorbike revving down the street,
My sister snoring in her crib,
Rain tapping on my window,
A ravenous robber eating chips and kebab,
Or . . .
A mad scientist blowing up a lab,
A wolf howling in the cemetery,
An Oompah loompa singing Gareth Gates,
A nan painting her nails pink,
But whatever it was, it's gone now.

Steven May (10)
Little London JMI School

Cry In The Night

It might have been . . .
Matilda reading books in her room,
The BFG making a noisy whizz popper
The Twits eating bird pie,
Mr Fox stealing a fat turkey,
Or . . .
James eating his giant peach with his friends,
The Oompah loompas singing opera,
My magic finger turning Mrs McKay into Macbeth,
Esio Trot trying to be a tortoise.
But . . .
Now they've all gone to bed *zzzzzz*.

Alexander Gibbons (10)
Little London JMI School

Cry In The Night

It might have been . . .
A wolf stepping on a twig in a dark alley,
My brother moaning in the bathroom,
Father Christmas climbing down the chimney,
A car's engine starting up in the road,
Or . . .
A dog in the garden, howling at the moon,
A frog eating cars in bed at twelve o'clock,
A dragon playing ping-pong with his sister,
An old man throwing eggs at a teenager down the street.
But now the sound has gone, I guess I'll never know what it was.

Lee Holmes (11)
Little London JMI School

Cry In The Night

It might have been . . .
A burglar stamping up the stairs,
A cat barking at the ugly mouse in the attic,
The monkey munching nuts in the jungle,
The ghost of David Beckham moaning in the shed,
Or . . .
My sister's friend eating dog food in the sitting room,
The owl eating the tree trunk in my back garden,
The teacher shouting at her son,
Oompah loompas singing opera,
But . . .
I'm not scared anymore
Good night, sleep tight, *zzzzzz*.

Perindi Patel (10)
Little London JMI School

A Cry In The Night

It might have been . . .
A wolf eating a rabbit in Sandwell Park,
An owl finding some food for his babies,
A dragon playing football with his brother,
An alien sitting on a bench killing people,
Or . . .
A frog eating cars and making a noise,
A drunken gang staggering down the street.

Jake Rackham (10)
Little London JMI School

The Witches' Poem

Quadruple, quadruple,
Sand and rubble,
Potion green and chocolate ripple.

Wingarda Leviosa turn this severed toe into a samosa
Then make something abominable appear even closer
Abominable Snowman's fluttering eyelid,
Then add a bin's lid.

Quadruple, quadruple,
Sand and rubble,
Potion green and chocolate ripple.

Toe of racoon,
That's put snakes in a saloon.
Eye of swan which was swimming in a pond
And not very fond.
Finger of shaven monkey
Who acts like he is funky.

Quadruple, quadruple,
Sand and rubble,
Potion green and chocolate ripple.

Corinne Collins (10)
Little London JMI School

The Witches' Cauldron

Double bubble foil and trouble
Fire burn and motor bubble
Massive leg, giant peg
Throw in quickly lizards' legs
Double bubble foil and trouble
Fire burn and motor bubble.

Joshua Lee (10)
Little London JMI School

The Witches' Cauldron

Triple, triple rest and sleep,
Death by chocolate and smelly feet.
Claw and tongue of mountain goat,
Leg of toad and smelly swamp.
Nose of turkey and add some goldfish lips smacking loudly.
Triple, triple rest and sleep
Death by chocolate and smelly feet.
Leg of Mark of little London
Ear of Shane from the zoo
And big, disgusting, dirty teeth.
Triple, triple rest and sleep
Death by chocolate and smelly feet.

Deonne Foster (10)
Little London JMI School

Nothing Spoke

A car parked at the kerb,
Like a stone statue
Kids practising their football skills
A lamp post flickers on and off
A green bin standing still
The pigeons pecking the food right off the floor
The winding road laying there still as a car goes down.

Jordan Farrell (9)
Little London JMI School

Nothing Spoke

Quiet, all but the sound of rain,
No sunbathers out today,
Ice cream vans driving away
And shopkeepers going home,
Donkeys walking around with their heads down,
Dolphins swimming away back home.

Harry Robinson (9)
Little London JMI School

Nothing Spoke

The night light flickered,
The children were asleep,
There were no people in the quiet street.

Nothing spoke.
The moon is out tonight,
The stars are glowing bright,
The sun is out of sight.

But then . . .
A child started screaming,
And parents started screeching,
An owl began hooting.

Lauren Dean (9)
Little London JMI School

Nothing Spoke

The sand was washed away with the gentle waves,
Small shells, big shells, seashells everywhere,
Dolphins jumping in and out of the deep blue sea.

But then . . .
The waves started crashing onto the sand
Pulling small shells, big shells out and away
Dolphins squeaking on their way home.

Ellie Beckett (9)
Little London JMI School

Nothing Spoke

A car came swiftly down the road.
A child was rushing down the pavement.
The builders chatted lightly on their lunch break.

Nothing spoke . . .
A pigeon munched on an apple.
The litter brushed along the street.
The wheel of the pushchair turned round and round.

But then . . .
The builders' tools crashed on the floor.
The car's horn went off.
The pushchair's bags fell to the floor.

Charlotte Brant (9)
Little London JMI School

Nothing Spoke

The spooky shadow on the bedroom wall,
The creaking of the garden gate,
The darkness mist in the sky.
Nothing spoke . . .
The spooky monster that lurks up high,
The children silent, almost dead
The ticking clock high up the wall,
But then . . .
The children jump up and shriek out loud
The darkness mist swooped in from
And the garden gate went *bang!*

Abigail Dudley (9)
Little London JMI School

Nothing Spoke

The whiteboard was shining
As the pencil snapped quietly.
The mouse was clicking.
The ruler was still and it did not move.
The teacher dreams of holidays.
Helpers are helping children do their maths.

Nothing spoke.
The water bottles shimmer into dark.
The desk creaking gently as though someone was touching it
As the trees tapped the windows.
Then the door opened gently.

But then . . .
The table became dusty
And the colouring pencils rolled off the teacher's desk
And the classroom came to life with the noise of the children.

Navneet Kaur (9)
Little London JMI School

Nothing Spoke

Nothing spoke.
The children sat quietly inside the house,
The car was parked still and soundless,
And the dog was standing like a statue silently.

Nothing spoke.
The man on the bicycle rode quietly,
The pigeons nibbled bread off the floor,
The bin stood still and noiseless.

But then . . .
The children started playing outside in the garden,
The dog barked loudly and boomed through the street,
The bicycle man rang his bell noisily.

Pavandeep Chanian (9)
Little London JMI School

Nothing Spoke

A strange looking woman walked slowly into the hairdressers,
An old pigeon swooped slowly past the window.

Nothing spoke.
A plate lay gently with soft juicy fruit on it,
A hairdryer lay quietly in the drawer,
The wind was brushing gently against the trees
Then . . .
The strange looking woman stomped her feet,
The old pigeon flew up into the sky,
The tray with the soft juicy fruit on it crashed onto the floor,
The hairdryer crashed and clanged against the bottles,
The wind blew the trees to one side.

Amelia Orme (9)
Little London JMI School

Nothing Spoke

Peace and quiet disturbed by twittering birds
People asleep start to stir.
They come outside and wave the birds away.
When they go back they get disturbed once again.

Nothing spoke.
People fast asleep.
Sleeping and dreams all so quiet and peaceful.

But then . . .
A cow in the field makes a big racket.
A cockerel in the farmyard says good morning
Then everyone wakes up and it's a beginning of a new day.

Balvinder Chopra (9)
Little London JMI School

Nothing Spoke

The ruler lays stiff and straight,
The water in the water bottle shimmers,
The pen waits to write,
The colouring pencil rolls off the table.

Nothing spoke.
The pencil lay under the table,
And the whiteboard shining white,
The sharpener ready to sharpen,
A piece of paper white and clean,
The dusty dictionary waiting to be read.

But then . . .
The ruler shaped,
The pen wrote
And the water bottle tipped over and the water poured out,
And the whiteboard had a maths question on it.

Rebecca Jassal (9)
Little London JMI School

Nothing Spoke

Nothing spoke.
The donkey trotted along gently,
The people sunbathed quietly,
And the shells stood still as the children played quietly.

Nothing spoke.
The dolphins swam under the sea quietly,
The crab snapped his claws silently
And the starfish made prints everywhere.

But then . . .
The dolphins splashed,
The sun glazed on the people
And the people chatted on and on.

Shannon Jackson (9)
Little London JMI School

Nothing Spoke

Nothing spoke.
The geese stood like statues
A man sat on a bench dreaming of a burger
A baby slept in a pushchair.

Nothing spoke.
The dog lay on a tree wondering what to do
A plant was in its seed
A window stood on a plank of wood.

But then . . .
The geese dashed in the water
And the man ran to his house
The window fell and smashed on the floor.

Daniel Khuttan (9)
Little London JMI School

Nothing Spoke

Nothing spoke.
The ruler lay straight on the table,
The rubber was cut straight in half,
The pen dried out because it had no lid.

Nothing spoke.
The chairs were just lying around,
The tables were all turned upside down,
The shaving of a pencil sitting on the ground.

But then . . .
The teacher told the children to tidy up,
The children made it even worse by throwing it all around,
The children could hardly walk around.

Mehal Patel (9)
Little London JMI School

Nothing Spoke

Nothing spoke.
The ruler lay on the blue, cold table.
The white dull board had maths questions on it.
The teacher's desk was scratched and dusty.
Nothing spoke.

The tree's branches tapped against the window.
The moon was swaying faster and faster.
The chairs stood with dust blowing off them.
But then . . .

The tapping of the branches got louder.
The moon was swaying faster and faster.
The chairs crashed against each other.

Amelia Hudson (9)
Little London JMI School

Nothing Spoke

Pigeons are peeking from the footpath,
Children are playing football,
Horses are pulling carts,
People are looking at their charts,
Horses are neighing loudly,
Children are standing proudly,
But then the sky is starting to get cloudy,
We should all go in,
A little girl has hurt her chin,
I came and helped with a grin.

Elle-Dee Martin (9)
Little London JMI School

Nothing Spoke

Fish and chips cooked to eat
It smells nice and tastes like meat
I find stones that I can keep
As I pick it up and look at it.
I have to leap on the rocks
To keep my feet nice and soft.
I go in the sea it is cold and freezes me
I swim around in the sea as I see someone doing the same as me
I have some candyfloss in my hand
It is sticky and it sticks on me
I jump in the sea and have a quick wash
I go in the water
I come back out and there is salt in my mouth
The sand is so soft it feels so good
As I lie down and see a boat.
I have a quick drink and it tastes like salt
I spit it out and start to feel ill.

Danielle Edwards (9)
Little London JMI School

Nothing Spoke

The rubbish flew about
The rubbish stood like a lazy gorilla
A rubbish bag hung on the roof.

Nothing spoke
The fence was wobbling like a piece of jelly
Two wheels were spinning in a circle
A four wheel bike was going around silently.

But then . . .
A wheel bin smashed together with a normal bin
A juggernaut was going off limit,
Went on a ramp and flew in the air
A bomb was set and blew up forty buildings.

Arun Virdi (9)
Little London JMI School

Poem

Football is exciting
Oh it's so fun!
Only the best players, get tired
When they *run! Run! Run!*
The ref blows his whistle as the ball goes out of play.
The ball goes off the pitch when the tackle is going down
All the people are screaming when they *score! Score! Score!*
We laugh after the match as we sing our footie songs
As they go like this,
'We are the champions, football is our game
We won three-two and they lost once again!'

Sean Savage (8)
Rednal Hill Junior School

The House Jungle

The kettle was whistling happily
The buzz of the TV as it comes alive
The chairs groaned as we sat on them
The tap cried tears all day long
The light winked as the bulb flew in circles
The sink gargled as the water swam down his long throat
The border of the fish tank keeps its face straight
The curtains kept their mouth open
The bath water ran a race to get to the top of the bath
The carpet lay fast asleep.

Lacey Bradford (11)
Rednal Hill Junior School

My Garden

I can see all the plants facing the sun
All the bulbs are opening up
The grass is short and wet from the rain last night
As it glistens and oh it gleams
All the cobwebs shine in the daylight sun
I feel safe and sound
No noise at all
All day long the flowers look pretty
I can hear the buzz of the bees collecting pollen
I smell the nice smell all around me
All the leaves are rattling together all day long
The same as the branches
The wind blows softly on the sunflowers.

Laura Hodgetts (8)
Rednal Hill Junior School

Joe Fairburn

J oe is my name
O ranges are my favourite fruits
E lephants are annoying.

F ish I have as pets
A my is my cute sister
I have ginger hair too
R abbits are very fussy
B ut I am different to those though
U niforms are rubbish
R aw carrots I hate
N ow it's time to say goodbye.

Joe Fairburn (8)
Rednal Hill Junior School

My Family

My family is great,
My family is fun,
We all work together,
Because there is lots to be done.

I have a big sister, who works away,
She travels the world from day to day,
I really miss her very much
But when she comes home
She makes a big fuss.

My mum and dad work very hard,
And I myself have a busy life.
I do, swimming, piano, dancing ballet
Tap, disco and gym.
It's very hard to fit it all in.

My dad is tall,
My mum is small,
But they are the best parents of all.

Tamara Gasteen (8)
Rednal Hill Junior School

Amy Fairburn

A my is my name,
M y friend is Marie,
Y ou can be my friend too.

F ish are my pets,
A pples are my favourite fruit,
 I am very sweet,
R abbits are my favourite pets,
B ut you are all I need,
U s friends can stick together,
R hubarb I like,
N ot as sweet as friends though.

Amy Fairburn (10)
Rednal Hill Junior School

Lifeguard

I can see people diving off the ledges.
I can feel water splashing all over me.
I can hear people shouting very loudly.
I can taste chlorine in the water.
I can smell chlorine in the air.
I hope and dream that nobody drowns.
I can see people splashing each other like the speed of lightning.
I can feel my heart beating when someone is drowning.
I can feel the heat of the swimming baths.
I can feel the vibration when the announcer says,
                              'The waves are coming on.'
I can hear the wave machine buzzing like a bumblebee
                                          buzzing loudly.
I can taste chlorine in the air because it is a disinfectant.
I hope that everybody enjoys themselves.

Liam Smith (10)
Rednal Hill Junior School

The Motorway Jungle

Cars zoom past
Like a cheetah running through the jungle.
People singing like strangled cats
Horns bibbing like anger running through someone's head.
Engines roaring like a fierce lion.
The peaceful road like an abandoned house.

Laura Mee
Rednal Hill Junior School

War

You can see dead, smelly bodies lying on the floor
Bullets zooming through the misty air
Soldiers dangerously fighting for their lives
And flames climbing up a building.

You can feel the force as a bomb explodes overhead
You can feel the bullets rattling under your feet
The vibration as a building falls down next to you
And you can feel the shock as a bullet hits your arm.

You can hear the shotguns as they bang and roar
Also you can hear a bomb explode and you think
                                        you are going to die
You can hear the mud squelching underneath your feet
And you can hear the soldiers screaming for their lives.

You can smell dead bodies rotting on the floor
Smoke when a bomb explodes
And you can smell the rations that the soldiers have left over.

Rhys Lewis (11)
Rednal Hill Junior School

Autumn Is The Best

Leaves are falling down on the frosty floor
Squirrels are around collecting acorns for autumn
They go inside ready to snuggle up in their warm beds
We are outside in our hats, coats, scarves, boots and gloves,
Kicking the leaves about.
All different coloured leaves flying in the sky
Then we go in to drink our warm milk and eat our tea,
We then go to bed and sleep.

Danielle Higgins (9)
Rednal Hill Junior School

The Football Match

I could see the footballers running on the wet
                          and slippery football pitch
I could see the fans on and off their seats
The referee showing the red card to a football player.

I could feel the excitement as a football player was
                          about to take a penalty.
I could feel the vibration as the crowd stamped their feet
                          on the ground.

I could hear the football being kicked.
The away fans singing songs,
And a footballer screaming as he went down hurt.

The taste of the rainy air made me feel so fresh.
I could taste the excitement as the match came to its final clash.
I could smell the hot dogs as the people ate,
I could smell the rainy grass of the football pitch
And the smoke of people smoking their cigars.

I hoped that the team that I was supporting would win.
I hoped that the hurt player was OK
And I dreamt of seeing another match like this.

Roman Pisnyy (10)
Rednal Hill Junior School

Autumn Poem

Autumn leaves are tumbling down,
Red, yellow, gold and brown,
It's cold and the sun hardly comes out
And all you do is shiver, shiver, shiver.
It's a good season for squirrels
And for them to collect acorns and nuts.
It's also a good season to collect conkers,
Some animals hibernate.
So just remember, autumn is a good season
So, which season do you like?

Kirsty Broomhall (9)
Rednal Hill Junior School

War

I can hear . . .
Ammo clinking from the machine guns in the tank,
The rockets from the cannon of the tank, *boom!*
Soldiers shouting, bellowing and getting their men in position,
Whistling of the bullets from the rifles going over
                                        the captains' heads.

I can see . . .
Flashes of guns like machine guns, rifles, sniper rifles,
Soldiers running here and there to get to cover,
Blood on the floor from dead soldiers,
Helicopters, tanks, jeeps, trucks dropping off men
                                        from the control centre.

I can feel . . .
The ground shaking below my feet as the grenade blows up,
The heat from the fires burning soldiers as it burns the ground,
Soldiers with rocket launchers destroying tanks, helicopters,
                                        jeeps, trucks,
And then it comes to a sudden stop as one country *wins!*

Ryan Harvey (10)
Rednal Hill Junior School

Autumn

Autumn leaves falling to the ground,
Make a rustling sound.
Beautiful colours
Red, green and golden brown.
Conkers fall on the ground
Just waiting to be found
Wrap up warm, winter's coming.

Jessica Bayliss (8)
Rednal Hill Junior School

Being A Lifeguard

I can see kids playing games,
As they make their sandcastles.
I can see dads taking their children surfing,
The kids are laughing and jumping.
I can see someone drowning!

I can feel the cold water on my toes,
As I swim to save the person.
I can feel the person is scared that they are drowning.

I can hear the person screaming as I get to her.
I can hear the splashing of the water,
As she tries to swim in a desperate attempt to find safety.

I can taste the saltwater in my mouth as I swim back to shore.
I can taste my tongue bubbling up
As an allergic reaction to the saltwater.

I can smell the fresh air as I sit on my chair again, sniffing the breeze.

Paige Campbell (10)
Rednal Hill Junior School

Brother Poem

B ehaves like a maniac when grown-ups aren't watching
R ampages most when you want to be quiet!
O rders you around as if you were his servant
T hinks of great ways to torment you
H ates above everything to hear you admired
E ats with loud noises just to irritate
R esorts to being charming only as the last desperate bribe.

Andrew Bilbrough (10)
Rednal Hill Junior School

The Beach

I can see the waves crashing against the grey rocks,
I can see other people building sandcastles
I can see children eating strawberry ice cream
I can see coloured seashells.

I can feel the freezing waves against my legs
I can feel the smooth, soft sand sliding through my hands
I can feel sunshine on my skin.

I can hear the screaming seagulls swaying in the sky
I can hear the sweet sea in the shells
I can hear children splashing in the sea.

I can taste strawberry ice cream as I eat it slowly
I can taste the salty saltwater as I swim through the sparkly waves
I can taste sandy sandwiches when the sand tumbles

from the towel.

I can smell salty water flowing in the air
I can smell burgers from the stands
I can smell the takeaway shops which makes my tummy rumble.

Stephanie Peay (10)
Rednal Hill Junior School

Carnival

See the clowns messing about,
Hear the children laugh and shout
Making you happy not sad
Making people feel glad
Party poppers going pop
Children laughing till they drop
The clunking noise of my boot
Squeeze my nose and hear it toot
Little children running around
Laughing and giggling to the sound.

Dean Sherrington (10)
Rednal Hill Junior School

Through A Rabbit's Eyes

Lush green meadows stretch out before me, an ocean of food.
A shimmering stream slithers through the green,
Water for my brothers and sisters to drink.
The wind whispers through the trees and bushes,
Cold on my ears, cooling me in the summer heat.
It carries the sound of nature, this is good.
I can detect predators on the singing wind.
My brothers and sisters gambol and tumble towards the stream.
They call me on the warm breeze; 'We've found a way across.'
We race through the stream,
Spray from their speed cools my face and tickles my whiskers.
They run into the field laughing.
I am not so sure,
I am upright, listening, ears twitching.
I smell something hot and evil on the wind from the trees,
Fear strikes me as I see a flash of red,
White, sharp teeth, piercing eyes rushing at them.
I scream, but no sound comes out, just the wind howling.
But my brothers and sisters are fast and agile.
With a spring and a flash of white tails they tear past me,
Racing for the safety of their burrows, I follow.
The stench of the fox's breath on my neck now.
The world turns to a green blur as I race for home.
Panting, exhausted, heart leaping I crash into the
                                    cool earth of my burrow.
I like days like this, I like being a rabbit.
I hope that the world doesn't change and that I stay this fast.
I hope the wind goes on singing and alerting me of danger.
I am a runner and a listener.
I am quicker than my enemies and I will play in the sun forever.

Marie Dipple (10)
Rednal Hill Junior School

The Blitz

I could hear the rat-a-tat of the automatic gun,
I fear that the next step I take could be my last,
Cold, wet mud was dripping down my neck when I hit the deck,
I was hoping that I would see my family again,
Freezing cold rain dribbling down my spine,
Gunfire coming from above and below,
Screams from pain and fear,
Jet planes were soaring through the sky,
I could smell smoke coming from jet planes above,
Spots of rain were tickling on my tongue,
I wish the war would end.

Reece Hales (10)
Rednal Hill Junior School

I'm A Soldier In The War!

Now I'm on the field, I see evacuees waving goodbye.
Dreaming and dreaming of mums and dads again.

I feel weak and unable to move.
I feel vibrations surging through my fingers and body.
The broken earth crumbles between my fingers.

Here I live in a hole in the ground.
I hear my team screaming as they run for cover.
I can almost taste their fear.
The smell of burning is everywhere as fires light up the sky.
I just want to go home.

Benjamin Bryans (10)
Rednal Hill Junior School

The Bowling Alley

One day I went bowling with my family
On my first shot I got a strike
We watched the ball roll down the alley
And then we looked for the score upon the screen
My little brother used the stand because he'd got a craggy hand.
We took it in turns to roll the ball.
Then my mom fell on the floor
All the balls were whizzing along,
And lots of people were singing a song.
You could feel the ball vibrating on the floor
Lots of people were coming through the door,
I got hungry so we had something to eat
That was a lovely treat; we then all took a seat.

Alex Childs (10)
Rednal Hill Junior School

The Bowling Alley

I can see a lot of different coloured balls knocking into all the pins,
I feel happy until my mom wins
And now I am sad and angry at the same time.
All I can hear is music and people laughing,
I can still taste my strawberry ice cream I've just eaten.
My chips must be done,
Well, I can smell them anyway,
I breathe the perfume of the lady who's walked past me.

Megan Gardner (10)
Rednal Hill Junior School

The Building Site

Diggers digging out trenches.
Big piles of bright red bricks that shine.
Wood and extremely large wagons carrying tiles and scaffolding.
You can feel the heat of the concrete and you can feel
                              the cold scaffolding poles.
The massive diggers reversing.
Disc-cutters chopping up the metal and concrete.
All you can taste is the sawdust in your mouth after the
                    chop saw has chopped through the wood.
You can smell the petrol of the machines
The smell of the rubble dust in the air.

Jordan Rush (10)
Rednal Hill Junior School

At The Swimming Baths

I'm in the swimming pool watching the float,
A rubber ring hovering like a large boat,
Excited children having swimming races,
The lifeguard doing up his laces,
Water splashing around their bodies
The waves are about to begin in
Five . . . four . . . three . . . two . . . one seconds
Waves hitting against you,
Swimming is good for you,
Chlorine that's what you can taste.

Sophie Savage (10)
Rednal Hill Junior School

My Class Pets

In my class we all have pets
And lots of pets we have,
Jill has a little mouse
Who she found on top of a hill.

In my class we all have pets
And lots of pets we have,
Bill says he has a pet pill
Who lives in his mom's mill.

In my class we all have pets
And lots of pets we have,
Lucy has a pet goose
Who's often on the loose.

In my class we all have pets
And lots of pets we have,
Zac has a pet cat
Who curls up on a mat.

In my class we all have pets
And lots of pets we have,
Finley has a pet blob
Who's known as a bit of a snob.

In my class we all have pets
And lots of pets we have,
Maisy has a pet daisy
Who can go a bit crazy.

In my class we all have pets
And lots of pets we have,
Katherine has a pet alien
Whose favourite word is 'or'.

Amy Griffiths (11)
Rednal Hill Junior School

The Blitz

I'm a soldier for Britain,
And I'm fighting in the war,
We're fighting in the war
And we want to show them the door.

I can see German bombers,
Who have destroyed our roads,
Bang, smash, hit and *boom,*
That's the Germans speaking in code!

Anger in my heart,
Excitement in my brain,
I'm getting very scared,
I feel like I'm going insane.

One of us has been shot down,
Now my mouth is dry,
Lots of people are dying,
Even people in the sky.

The sirens are screeching,
People are starting to cry,
Now I'm starting to worry,
What if I were to die?

The noises have finished coming,
Yes, yes we have won,
But look at our city,
What have they done?

Laura Stonehall (10)
Rednal Hill Junior School

The Forest

The forest is very windy and very cold.
Leaves are falling off the trees.
I can hear lots of wolves howling
And the rain hitting the ground like a firework in the sky.
I can hear water hitting my head.
The taste of the forest and the smell of the wind.
The horrible smell of the smoke coming from big trees.
I can see ducks swimming away to their homes
and people playing golf.
I do hope it will stop raining and the sun will come out
And then I can sunbathe all day.

Shannon Danks (10)
Rednal Hill Junior School

Sunshine

The sunshine is an angel
The sunshine is a surgeon
Making people prettier and tanned
Shouldn't ever stop
Talking to the birds and the bees way up high.

The sunshine is happiness
Smiling down at you, when you need a friend
Taking your thoughts away
The sunshine is love and laughter
Bringing joy every day.

Terri Smith (10)
Rednal Hill Junior School

At The Hippodrome

The red curtains are closed like a young rose,
I feel excited and happy as though I'm a real dancer,
The music is playing loudly like one hundred musicians
I smell the old curtains, they're like musty clothes
                              that have been thrown away,
The curtains open and dancers twirl around the stage
                              like birds in the sky,
I wonder what's going to happen next?
The sound of the dancers' movement washes over me,
The red curtains close and open again,
Now I feel as proud as a peacock,
All I can hear now are people clapping,
I hope I become a dancer when I'm older.

Meghan Finn (10)
Rednal Hill Junior School

On The Beach

As I walk along the burning sand
I see the surfers splashing up the waves.
The ice cream van's song as it vibrates through the sand
                              as I sit on a beach towel.
Children screaming when seaweed gets stuck
                              in-between their toes.
As I sit I feel the sun burning my skin as I fall asleep.
When I wake I am freezing as a bucket of water is tipped over me.
I run toward the colourful van which says *Hot Dogs*
                              as they sizzle on the hot cooker
But there is one thing I hope will still be here . . .
The beach.

Jessica Pearson (10)
Rednal Hill Junior School

The Eagle

As the eagle steps off the branch it breaks the sunlight
It starts to swoop in the air across fields and towns,
The eagle spots its prey
A tiny mouse scurrying away to save its life,
The eagle breaks its back.
The powerful eagle swoops loop to loop and finally
                                              lands on the earth.
The eagle's vision goes sharp again looking for the tiny mouse.
As the eagle is silent it gently takes off again,
Drifting above the forest canopy, for then it loses the mouse.
The eagle starts surging back off into the air and forward
                                              towards the sun.
As its beauty reflects a shadow on the ground large enough
                                              for the town to see.
The eagle swoops back into the sky and vanishes for no one to see.

Reece Hawley (10)
Rednal Hill Junior School

My Pets

My cat Ginger is a whinger
He is only a kitten, but has already bitten.

My fish is golden and rather olden
He gets in a mood if he does not get his food.

My dog is called Lottie but is not a Scottie
He is rather flirty and his paws always get dirty.

My hamster was called Louise and had not got fleas
One night in bed she ate my fleece and we never got any peace.

My bunny called Honey loves it when it's sunny
He loves having fun in his run.

My gerbil called Paige loves to come out of her cage.
She is rather fat and does not like our cat.

Hannah Branch (10)
Rednal Hill Junior School

The Fairground

Children screaming
People shouting
The ghost trains roar
Babies crying to go home.

The roller coasters dip
Rolling down the track
People buying candyfloss
People bashing into each other on the bumper cars
Children sliding down the helter-skelter.

I can smell the smell of candyfloss
Stink bombs going off.

I can feel the crash of the bumper cars
The sickness of the roller coaster.

Reece Watters (10)
Rednal Hill Junior School

The Days Of The Week

On Monday I can see children playing happily.
On Tuesday I feel different things in science.
On Wednesday I hear different things to help me learn.
On Thursday I enjoy pie.
On Friday I have lots of fun choosing a new book in the library.
Every day I have lots of fun doing different subjects.

Henry Mupanemunda (7)
Ruckleigh School

Seasons

Autumn
Green leaves turning brown,
Yellow, red and crisp,
Smell the fresh fruit growing on the trees.
Conkers falling on my head.
Leaves crushing under my feet
Fog as white as snow.

Winter
Trees bare except evergreens,
I can see my breath a grey and white colour,
I can taste the snow on my tongue,
I am shivering in my boots.

Spring
Trees in blossom giving people hay fever,
Starting to get warm again,
People taking off their scarves,
Baby animals being born.

Summer
People are playing in gardens and parks,
You can hear lawnmowers mowing the lawn in the distance
Smell the barbecues with beef, chicken and pork,
Hear the birds tweet.

I love how the seasons are different from each other!

Laura Newboult (10)
Ruckleigh School

Spring

In spring you can hear the chirping of a baby bird
And the happy cheers of the children.
You can smell the lavender and the sap from the trees.
You can see eggs ready to hatch
And lots of squirrels with ducklings in the pond.
You can touch the flowers.
Summer comes but that is another poem!

Nicholas Marshall (7)
Ruckleigh School

To Travel The World

To feel the sand in Spain
To feel the fear on the rides in America
To touch Victoria Falls and to feel the water rushing down on you
To smell the fresh blossoms blooming on the trees in Berlin
To see the children's laughter whilst playing in London
To taste the different food in all sorts of countries
To hear the band playing at the festival in China
To finally get home and relax
And to think how much fun we've had.
To see how much laughter we had in my garden
And then to see the rainbow shooting across the sky
And just think how lucky you are to have a family
                                    to love and to care for.
But then in a week you're on the plane again
To travel the world a bit more and that day comes
To taste the fruit growing on the trees in Portugal
And smell the smell that you've never smelt before
At a place you have always dreamt of but you could never go there.

Nancy Foote (11)
Ruckleigh School

Autumn Comes

Autumn comes with blowing trees,
Also with a slight breeze,
Twizzling branches from the trees,
With the falling leaves,
Slight sun comes between the lovely breeze,
Green trees dancing in the lovely breeze,
Feeling rusty as can be,
While the dust feels a breeze,
Hearing the old trees!

Abir Iqbal (8)
Ruckleigh School

The Unicorn

I am sure I saw a unicorn,
When I went for a walk in the wood,
I am sure I saw a unicorn,
Glowing as it should.

I am sure I saw a unicorn,
Glimmering, glinting, glittering,
I am sure I saw a unicorn,
Shining, silvery, shimmering.

I am sure I saw a unicorn,
Like it was in a book,
I am sure I saw a unicorn,
So I told my sister to look.

I am sure I saw a unicorn,
And my sister saw it too,
I am sure I saw a unicorn,
So why will no one believe me . . . do you?

Lydia Bullivant (10)
Ruckleigh School

Food

I can see lots of food
Chips and fruit on a long table
Lots of food in a long line
I can smell lots and lots of chocolate
Chips, cakes and yummy cream buns.
I can hear people munching on
Pizza and carrots and oranges.
I am looking on the table.
Yummy, I have a big rumble in my tummy
From all the food on the table.

Camani Lall (7)
Ruckleigh School

The Best Holiday Ever

The smell of the sea water,
The taste of the salt.
I could hear the waves,
The swaying of the rustling palm trees.
My dog running through the sand,
Scaring the seagulls away!

The feeling inside me
How happy I am!
My dog was swimming,
We were playing catch.

It started to rain,
We decided to go.
In the car the dog jumped on me,
He sat on me the whole way home!
I was so exhausted
When we got home.
Sad that I was no longer on holiday.
I went straight to bed.

Zoe Harding (10)
Ruckleigh School

I Am A Boy

I am a boy by my friend.
My friend and I are really good friends.
We like to share everything.
We love to play football.
We like to play netball.
That is what a boy's life is like.
We like to play cricket.
We like to skip and most of all we all like homework!

Isa Danyal Zaman (7)
Ruckleigh School

School

School may not be cool,
You might think it's a waste of time,
But in fact it's the only place where you play with your mates.

You and I see children working,
But they're not; they're talking about the latest games!

When you work you can feel the teacher is looking at you,
But she's not looking at you,
She's looking at the person next to you,
You cannot do what you want to do!

You may not hear anything,
But when it is playtime,
You can hear the whole of England
It's the noisiest place in the world!

You may not smell much,
But when it is dinner time,
You smell the loveliest thing in the world,
When you eat it, it's like eating the Queen's meal.

Hamza Rafiq (11)
Ruckleigh School

Buzzy Bee

I can hear a bee buzzing above my head.
I try not to move.
I stay as still as a tree.
I can feel its wings touching my head.
I can see its black and yellow stripes
And I'm sure it's a bee.
I hope it does not sting me!
Ouch!

Grace Eyles (7)
Ruckleigh School

Grace The Christmas Cat

(In the style of Benjamin Zephania)

Grace wakes up
Yawns
Leaps towards the stairs
Turns into the lounge
Collides into the Christmas tree
And sleeps
Grace wakes
Stretches
Bangs her head on the Christmas tree
Sets her eyes on a ribbon
Pounces towards it
And misses!
Grace snuggles on a cushion
Then sleeps
Grace wakes
Looks around
Goes outside, then comes back in
Enters the kitchen
Tears the turkey
Stalks out of the room
Back to the garden
Burrows under the snowman
And sleeps.

Caroline Camm (8)
Ruckleigh School

My Pet

I have a cat
A fat cat
And this is why he's fat
Because he eats the carpet
He chews and chews and chews.
His teeth are sharp
And if he bites
It will really hurt.

Mason Gain (7)
Ruckleigh School

The Horror Of World War II

I'm standing in the cold, wet trench,
With the waves of the radio blaring.
The chattering of the machine guns,
The heavy tanks rolling across the ground.
Medics running to the injured!
The cold metal of my machine gun on my skin.
My heavy equipment on my back,
I can just see over the trench wall
And people are being taken prisoner.
I feel scared and want to go home,
Worried about dying!
I thought the war was pointless,
Now I know it was!

Callum Williamson (10)
Ruckleigh School

My Teacher Thinks I'm . . .

My teacher thinks I'm listening to her but I'm not,
I'm riding on a shark's back in the Pacific Ocean.
My teacher thinks I'm writing but I'm not,
I'm Hercules fighting a three-headed dragon with purple scales.
My teacher thinks I'm reading but I'm not,
I'm in a spaceship in space finding DNA traces of aliens.
My teacher thinks I'm working but I'm not,
I'm skiing in snowy Alaska.
So my teacher thinks I'm listening, writing reading and working,
But I'm daydreaming.

Shyam Kotecha (10)
Ruckleigh School

Soldier At War

S our guilt as the first gun fires.
O ver the hill, people crying.
L ower and lower the first soldier falls
D own and down the first bullet falls.
 I n the flesh bringing pain and gore.
E arly days early nights, bringing pain, gore and fright.
R ealising the pain falls down dead with guilt and shame.

A fraid children huddled up
T error hits the streets bringing shock

W ailing mother, afraid for her child.
A way they flee for the city.
R oaring gun fires in the village.

Do you think it will ever finish?

Katie Cogley (10)
Ruckleigh School

My Very Own Pet

P ets being bought, pets being sold,
E very pet playing with one another,
T alking to one another, having communication with one another.

S mells, funny smells like the dog's leather collar.
H orrid smells, you don't want to know about!
O n tables, in cages and in boxes are the animals
P lease Mummy, let me have a hamster!

Karina Gahir (10)
Ruckleigh School

Polo The Christmas Cat

(In the style of Benjamin Zephania)

Polo wakes up
Licks his paws
Rolls around
And runs up the Christmas tree
Knocks the angel off the top
Falls forwards
Gingerly gets up
Pads along the corridor
Snoozes.
Polo wakes up
Yawns
Stretches
Falls down the stairs
Runs outside
And races straight into a snowman
He sprints into the house
And sleeps.
Polo wakes
Stalks some white mice into the kitchen
Spots mince pies
Gobbles them all up
And sleeps.

Katherine Hateley (9)
Ruckleigh School

Soldiers

You can see men and the dens
You can hear the drills and the planes
You can feel sadness all around you
And the pain.

Harry Simmons (7)
Ruckleigh School

Pudding The Christmas Cat

(In the style of Benjamin Zephania)

Pudding wakes up
Pads around his mat
Leaps onto the fireplace
Devours the stocking
Curls into a ball
And sleeps.
Pudding opens an eye
Prowls down the stairs
Gobbles the Christmas pudding
And sleeps.
Pudding wakes
Rips open his presents
Demolishes the sparkling tinsel
Stalks round in circles
And sleeps.
Pudding wakes up
Feasts on succulent turkey
Leaps onto a mouse
Darts down the corridor
Curls onto the TV
And sleeps.

Grace Mupanemunda (9)
Ruckleigh School

Autumn Sunshine

Sunshine is a light glowing in mid-air.
It will always follow me wherever I go.
It is in a sky filled with autumn colours.
I can hear birds singing a tuneful song.
Trees are swaying side to side.
Raindrops are sliding off the trees
And dribbling down my neck.

Zoe Quinn (10)
Ruckleigh School

My Magic, Beautiful Box

(Based on 'Magic Box' by Kit Wright)

I shall put in my box . . .
All the love I have.
A beautiful sunset
And some beautiful crystals.

I shall put in my box . . .
All the secrets I have,
A special wish
And the love from my parents.

I shall put in my box . . .
Beautiful dreams
And another dream that may come true,
Also a photo of my lovely parents.

My box will have diamonds shaped of hearts all over it.
My box will have beautiful patterns made with gold.

In my box I will float on a cloud . . .
Made of soft feathers
And fall into a deep, deep sleep
And wake up to see more of my box.

Alexandra Cheung (10)
Ruckleigh School

On Top Of A Mountain

I have just climbed a massive mountain,
I can see the clouds drifting by,
The sunrise is pretty and bright,
It is a crisp, cold, damp morning,
I am freezing cold and worn out,
There is a lot of snow up here.

The birds are tweeting merrily,
I am just about to clamber down,
I cannot wait to see my family and be in familiar surroundings again.

Katie Smith (10)
Ruckleigh School

Crystal The Christmas Cat

(In the style of Benjamin Zephania)

Crystal wakes up
Yawns
Remembers the date
Pads downstairs
Eats
Naps.
Crystal wakes up
Plays with the tinsel
Pounces on the decorations
Dances under the fairy lights
Pins the ribbons on her ears
Eats
Drowses.
Crystal wakes up
Rushes to the garden
Darts in and out of the snow
Scampers with next-door's kitten
Sniffs the mince pies
Licks the turkey
Sleeps cosily.

Muskan Shrivastava (9)
Ruckleigh School

The Amazing Run

At the door I jump down,
Through the air towards the ground,
I pull the parachute and fly up high,
And land safely with a sigh.

I run towards the trench,
As I passed I saw the dead,
Dodging bullets I run and run,
I make a jump for the trench,
But someone shoots me dead.

Samuel Maguire (10)
Ruckleigh School

A Mother At War

The noise made by the battle,
Goes rattle, rattle, rattle.
A shelter is all we need,
Because they are in the lead.
In the house we are so cold
We have nothing left to hold.
I think I'm a good mother,
All I can do is cover.
We would try to scarper,
But, I'm so filled with anger!
We're both so terrified,
All the guns are being fired!
Booming bombs of black,
Firing flames of fluorescent fire!
Now, I'm beginning to tire.

Pauline Rowsome (10)
Ruckleigh School

Wars!

Soldier scarer,
Bunker bomber,
Sword scraper,
Flame fighter,
Enemy eradicator,
Death bringer,
Cigar smoker,
Gory grenadier,
Black bayonet,
Soulless soldiers.

Marcus Rhodes (10)
Ruckleigh School

My Magic Box

(Based on 'Magic Box' by Kit Wright)

I would put in my box . . .
A pinch of happy emotion,
An everlasting meal,
A genie in a lamp.

I would put in my box . . .
A wizard who makes planets,
A spaceship from the future,
A key with magical powers.

I would put in my box . . .
A teaspoon of gold dust,
A fragment of a rainbow,
A sprig of ancient oak.

My box would be made from clouds and ivory,
Embossed with ancient patterns,
With mother of pearl and silver.

In my box I would go to faraway lands,
Go to whole worlds of chocolate and sweets
And travel the universe.

Edward Maclean (9)
Ruckleigh School

Sweets!

S weets, sweets, oh lovely sweets,
W e have them all the time,
E ach day I smell them past the meats,
E ach sweet tastes, just fine!
T reats each week oh such delight
S oon it's the dentist, we'll have a fright!

Francesca Dunn (10)
Ruckleigh School

My Magic Box
(Based on 'Magic Box' by Kit Wright)

I would put in my box . . .
A piece of joy
And the world's best ploy
And of course the world's best clocks.

In my box you would find . . .
A dragon's golden hind
A crown of an earl
And a shield encrusted with pearl.

I would put in my box . . .
A man's first fire
Apollo's lyre
From Greek times long ago.

My box will be made of
The finest oak
Encrusted with every jewel
Covered by a magic cloak.

I would take my box everywhere
Taking great care
No damage may come to it
At my death it will go in a pit.

Sam Bennett (10)
Ruckleigh School

The Wicked War

I'm in the war,
And my feet are sore.
On the battlefield,
With my sword and shield.

I'm in the war,
I hate blood and gore.
I bombed a bay,
Then ran away.

Andrew Dillon (10)
Ruckleigh School

My Magic Box

(Based on 'Magic Box' by Kit Wright)

I would put in my box . . .
A breath of fresh air from the ocean shore,
A forest of dreams
And lots, lots more.

I would put in my box . . .
Golden silk from the Queen's robe,
All the pearls of Persia
And all the knowledge of the globe.

I would put in my box . . .
Some peacock's feathers,
My favourite teddy
And some of the finest leathers.

My box would be carved of oak
And laid with gold leaf too,
On the outside it would have woven silk
It would be the size of my shoe.

I would take my box around the world twice
I would take my box to the Isle of Skye,
Then I would put it back on my shelf.

Katherine Bridges (9)
Ruckleigh School

Snake

Slowly, silently
Up the tree trunk vines
A scary scaly creature appears
Slithering from left to right
It disappears
Again into
The dark night.

Elise Flaherty (11)
Ruckleigh School

My Magic Box

(Based on 'Magic Box' by Kit Wright)

I would put in my box . . .
A crystal from the highest mountain in the world
Some shells from Turkey
A piece of cloud.

I would put in my box . . .
An everlasting story,
A magical fairy
A piece of the Eiffel Tower.

I would put in my box . . .
The happiest poem in the world,
A crystal ball to tell me my future,
A picture of my family,
A lump of sand from Egypt.

My box will be formed from a weeping willow
With a beautiful princess with crystals on
On the inside of the lid would be golden silk
Some wishes of my own on the side.

I would surf the world in my box
I would slowly drift to the peaceful places
Then slowly go to Heaven
After sleeping on the roof on the world.

Sarah Habib (9)
Ruckleigh School

My Magic Box

(Based on 'Magic Box' by Kit Wright)

I would put in my box . . .
A crimson crystal,
A well of wonderful wishes
And a chunk of care.

I would put in my box . . .
A dreamy cloud with a silver lining,
A blue balloon
And a thought of peace with scrumptious love.

I would put in my box . . .
A clear conscience
With a feeling of an angel
And some love from my mum.

My box is made of platinum and
Love carved on the top.
Inside my box is a layer of friendship
With a large hug on top.

My box and I would fly the world
Up, up to the sun
And sleep there until we were ninety-one
And come back down from the sun.

Sophie Foxon (9)
Ruckleigh School

My Magic Box
(Based on 'Magic Box' by Kit Wright)

I would put in my box . . .
The root of a tree,
The sound of the sea,
A grain of golden sand.

I would put in my box . . .
The crash of the sea against the cliffs,
The bark of an ancient oak,
A piece of golden silk.

I would put in my box . . .
A glistening ruby,
The first light of the sun,
A new flower.

My box would be made of
Ancient oak wood.
The hinges would be gold
And the inside would be silver.

I would take my box around the world,
And sail to a new country.

Edward Evans (9)
Ruckleigh School

My Magic Box
(Based on 'Magic Box' by Kit Wright)

My magic box is a lovely place to be,
It has so many things to see like,
Crystal stones and marbles too,
Special places that I can dream,
Wishes are spoken in each corner of my box.

Special things that I got from holiday in my box,
Noises from outside like ducks quaking,
Dogs barking, drums banging.
On the lid of my box is amazing stuff
As in tigers, birds, lions too especially . . . *dogs!*

Lucy Ingleston (9)
Ruckleigh School

My Magic Box

(Based on 'Magic Box' by Kit Wright)

I would put in my box . . .
A golden glass from the British Isles,
A diamond from Australia
And some gold coins in piles.

I would put in my box . . .
The hottest flame of the world
The loudest bell in England,
Some golden string that's curled.

I would put in my box . . .
A giant iron sword,
Green, red and blue dragons
And of course a secret word.

My box would stay on an earth
I hope that it would fit!
It would stay there for years and years,
Just waiting for someone to find it.

Marcus Powis (9)
Ruckleigh School

My Magic Box

(Based on 'Magic Box' by Kit Wright)

I would put in my box . . .
Lots of wishes
And a lump of love
And the sunset shining on the sea.

I would put in my box . . .
Fresh clean water
And some snowflakes and ice.

I would put in my box . . .
A football match
And I would fly up to Heaven.

Hasan Shareef (9)
Ruckleigh School

My Magic Box

(Based on 'Magic Box' by Kit Wright)

I would put in my box . . .
A thousand gifts which are wrapped and ready to open.
I would put in a cluster of stars and diamonds,
Some leaves from an autumn tree.

I would put in my box . . .
The brightest sunshine ever.
I would put all my memories from my holidays
So I will never forget them.

I would put in my box . . .
A dog or a cat.
Some pictures of my family,
Some colourful seashells
And a brilliant book with beautiful pictures.

My box would be made of strong wood
And it would be painted gold.
The lid would be covered in stars,
Inside would be picture of friends
And pictures of animals too.

I would travel to every corner of the world.
I would see the pyramids of Egypt.
Then I would come back to my home
And search the world again and again until I get tired.

Shreeya Kotecha (9)
Ruckleigh School

My Magic Box

(Based on 'Magic Box' by Kit Wright)

I will put in my box . . .
Crystals and jewels and a beautiful roar of the sea,
A seashell from Spain,
A dog and some birds
And my mum's warm hands.

I will put in my box . . .
Teddies and toys and maybe some chocolate bars.
Some pretty, kind words,
My favourite people
And a tiny lion cub.

I will put in my box . . .
Miss Skidmore and Lucy, Katherine and Shreeya.
My favourite fruits such as bananas and apples
And also 'Hello Kitty!'
My aunties Kate and Emma, who are so kind.

My box would be aqua and lilac,
A funny oval shape
With flowers, hearts, moons and stars all over it.

I would tour the world and far beyond
All with my magic box.
I would fly over the rainbow
And over the stars
And safely back again.

Autumn Roberts (9)
Ruckleigh School

My Magic Box

(Based on 'Magic Box' by Kit Wright)

I would put in my box . . .
A hair from a dog,
Pebbles from a beach in Greece
And a star from the sky.

I would put in my box . . .
A flame from a fire,
A piece of snow from Christmas
And a mysterious surprise.

I would put in my box . . .
Cleansing water from a stream,
Poems from the greatest author
And family happiness.

My box would be golden with stars,
It would have amazing wishes in each star,
It would have my name printed on it with wood
And it would have a tiny ballerina twirling inside.

I would shrink and dance with the ballerina,
I would sit in the soft pebbles
And I would softly fall asleep.

Shona Williamson (9)
Ruckleigh School

My Magic Box

(Based on 'Magic Box' by Kit Wright)

I would put in my box . . .
All my family and friends,
A handful of stars to light up the lid
And a few bottles of water to drink.

I would put in my box . . .
A ton of gold to share,
A big loving heart
And twenty comfortable beds to sleep on.

I would put in my box . . .
A few little fishes,
A happy yellow sun
And some of the world's most endangered animals.

My box would be made of silver,
With the stars glittering,
Until no more could go in.

I would live in my box till the end of day
And when it came we would snuggle down
Until we were awoken.

Charles Badham (9)
Ruckleigh School

My Magic Box

(Based on 'Magic Box' by Kit Wright)

I would put in my box . . .
Some water, as clean as can be.
Rare plants from Madagascar
And a piece of gold.

I would put in my box . . .
A powerful wave,
A red amulet
And the coldest ice in the world.

I would put in my box . . .
My pet fishes,
Sand sculptures from Cornwall,
The happiest poem in the world.

My box would be made from crystal
With golden sides,
A surprise at the bottom
And the lid would be silver.

I would fly in my box
High above the clouds
And I would fly around the world.

Richard Miller (9)
Ruckleigh School

My Magic Box

(Based on 'Magic Box' by Kit Wright)

I would put in my box . . .
A piece of extra life
And the sun from Menorca.

I would put in my box . . .
My eldest dog's heart
And the sand from the calmest beach.

I would put in my box . . .
A moment of sadness to remember my great-grandpa
And my dead dog Coco.

My box would be made of happiness and sadness,
Some wood made by my grandpa
And some sparkling silver glitter.

I would play cricket for Warwickshire,
Go to America
And I would wish all my family alive again in my box.

Lawrence Finch (9)
Ruckleigh School

Autumn

A utumn is the time when animals hibernate.
U p in the trees there are conkers falling.
T he leaves are turning lovely colours, red, yellow,
                              orange, gold, bronze.
U p in the trees are spiders in their webs.
M isty, foggy mornings this time of year.
N ights are darker and longer too.

Samuel Russell (7)
St Benedict Biscop Primary School, Wombourne

My Family

My family is the best,
Better than all the rest,
All day in and all day out,
I want you to scream and shout!

My sister is a nutter,
She is slippy just like butter.
She is annoying and a real pain,
Oh, I wish I had a cane!

Now, my dad is really funny,
And over to me I'm a real dummy.
My dad is very clever,
Me, never.

My mum loves to scream and shop,
When she shouts at me, my ears go *pop*!
Everything she buys every day,
I think, *wow, what a lot to pay!*

Me and my cousins, we always have fun,
We love sausages in bun.
Me and my cousin, I love everything we do,
We always play something new.

That was my family they're really great,
All my friends and my very best mate!
My family is the best,
Better than all the rest!

Thomas Kiely (10)
St Benedict Biscop Primary School, Wombourne

Zoo

There was an old man of Cud-oo
Who went to the zoo at nearly two
When he came out
He'd broken his back
By getting in the way of an emu!

Sam Greensill (9)
St Benedict Biscop Primary School, Wombourne

The Sunny Beach

Stretched out sleepily in the shade
On a day when the sun's as fierce as a ball of burning fire.
I'm feeling really hot and sticky
And my face is as red as a bright lobster.

The sea looks like glistening diamonds
As I head towards it for a swim.
But the sand burns my feet like they're on fire
Making me run as fast as my blistered feet have ever run before.

I'm so glad to reach the water
I splash about like a mad hooligan.
The tiny waves welcome me like a cool breeze
And feel as cool as ice.

I then play happily in the sun
As cool as the fridge.
I then sunbathe in the sun
Like a baby fast asleep.

Emma Jones (10)
St Benedict Biscop Primary School, Wombourne

Autumn

A utumn leaves falling down off the tree
U p in the tree the squirrels store nuts
T he cobwebs hang on the tree
U p in the sky birds go to the sun
M ore hedgehogs gather their food
N ext morning there is a robin in the sky.

Charlotte Jones (7)
St Benedict Biscop Primary School, Wombourne

At The Horse Race

As the riders mount their horse,
They look over the course.
As they're led into the gates,
The horses say hello to their mates.

There they go into the race,
They pick up on a steady pace.
Look at their hooves digging into the ground,
Their manes swishing all around.

Imagine if you could ride,
Instead of standing at the side.
Cameras flashing and people screaming,
Others smiling and beaming.

If you've placed a bet will you be upset?
Imagine if you've won the bet.
Smell the air,
They're nearly there!

First, second and third,
I hope your horse keeps their word.
Your horse has won the race!
A big smile spread across your face!

Georgina Taylor (10)
St Benedict Biscop Primary School, Wombourne

Autumn

A t autumn I love to watch the gold leaves
                            fall down from the shorter trees
U sually the big conkers come off the tall trees
T he big leaves fall off the trees with the conkers
                                in their prickly shells
U p in the trees you cannot see a lot of leaves
M erry Christmas is almost here everyone
N uts are getting eaten by the squirrels at night.

Joshua Rogers (7)
St Benedict Biscop Primary School, Wombourne

The Storm

The wild storm rages like an angry giant.
Flashing lightning bolts through the sky like fiery weapons.
The wind shrieks violently like a strangled cat
As its thunderous voice screams and echoes furiously.
The icy touch gripped the house as tightly as a leather belt.
The rain beats furiously against the window like smashing glass.
Inside, the fire greets us like I'm thawing out a piece of bread
And we feel as warm and snug as a spider in its web.
The warmth of my home is like a boiling hot bath.
I look out the window and the storm is growing worse.
I walk outside and the hail is like ping-pong balls on my head.

Amy Wright (11)
St Benedict Biscop Primary School, Wombourne

Autumn

A utumn is coming!
U nderground animals are hibernating ready for the winter
T he brown trees are losing their shiny leaves
U sually happy children are picking the shiny round conkers
off the tall trees with the golden, orange and yellow leaves
M y small garden is covered in golden red leaves
instead of shiny green grass
N uts are covering the pavement while the squirrels
are picking them.

Jordan Brindley (7)
St Benedict Biscop Primary School, Wombourne

The Storm

The wild storm rages like an angry giant,
Bright and fierce lightning bolts through the sky like fiery weapons.
As its thunderous voice explodes furiously
The wind shrieks angry like a hurricane.
The icy snow drops grip the houses as tightly as possible.
The rain beats furiously against the windows
                        like a boxer hitting you.
The fire greets us like an important man and we feel warm.
People try to get to bed but the noise is waking them up.
The rain is stopping.
The thunderous thunder hasn't been heard since ten o'clock.
The clouds are clear, stars are shining bright
And people are going asleep.

Zach Wright (10)
St Benedict Biscop Primary School, Wombourne

The Storm

The wild storm rages like an angry giant,
Flashing frightening lightning bolts through the sky like fiery weapons
As its thunderous voice roars like an angry lion and echoes furiously.
The wind shrieks almost deafening like a plague of mice
                        running for their lives.
Its icy frozen drops grip the house as tightly as an old oak tree.
The rain beats furiously against the windows like
                    someone banging a table.
Inside the fire greets us like the sun
And we feel as warm as a fly wrapped in a spider's web.

Christina Westwood (10)
St Benedict Biscop Primary School, Wombourne

The Snowy Garden

The garden cuddles under a blanket of snow,
The snow hides the grass, covering it from the warning cold.
A garden fence stands to attention still despite the snow,
Snow dominates the trees covering it in a white blank substance.
Wind screams against the window which is braving the snowing.
Snow rolls down the grass which is facing extinction.
Who would dare mention the ice, glinting, hiding, waiting to grow.
Who would dare mention the beaten battlefield which saw snow
Defeat the star-struck garden.

Stanley Howell (10)
St Benedict Biscop Primary School, Wombourne

Autumn

A nimals hibernating and birds migrating
U sual cold winds blasting by
T he spiky conker shells and red and bronze leaves dropping
                         down to the floor from the bushy trees
U ncle Frank gathering the leaves into a pile on the grass
M yself jumping into the pile of colourful leaves
N uts round the green bushy trees for the squirrels to get.

Rebecca Luter (7)
St Benedict Biscop Primary School, Wombourne

Autumn

A ll the conkers falling off the waving trees
U sually the leaves are falling off the trees and softly blowing down
T he spiders are making webs in the hedge
U sually the wind is blasting by
M y uncle David helps me get the conkers
N early the time when the birds fly away and more animals hibernate.

James Keogh (7)
St Benedict Biscop Primary School, Wombourne

Midnight Mayhem

I ran through the night pursued from behind
Hopes and dreams, rush through my mind.
I turned around to see where it was, but where did it go?
I looked down the cliff and it was hiding below.

I turned and ran, darting left and right,
Into the darkness and into the night.
Exhausted and tired I fell in the grit,
I listened hard; I thought I'd lost it.

I looked on ahead and there was a hut,
I ran straight ahead but the door was locked shut.
I'd given up hope with a pain in my back,
I leant on the door and waited for attack.

I saw it come at me, ready to glide,
And just as it swooped, the door opened wide.
I looked up at a welcoming face
I stood up and found myself in a primitive place.

There I was, there were pots on the fire,
In the corner of the room the man sat on a dirty old tyre.
I could hear the creature scratching at the door,
I knew he'd get through, that was for sure.

It burst through the door and clawed the man,
I tried to help him by throwing pots and pans.
I picked up a shotgun and aimed at his head,
I pulled the trigger and he ate hot lead!

James Randall (10)
St Benedict Biscop Primary School, Wombourne

Chicken

There was an old man of St Bees
He had a great pal from St Cleeves
They decided to eat a chicken
It tasted finger-lickin'
At the end of the meal they had grease on their sleeves.

Mitchell Jordan (9)
St Benedict Biscop Primary School, Wombourne

My Pets

I have a very lazy dog,
Most of the time he sleeps like a log.
He is very friendly and would never fight
In fact if he sees an Alsatian he trembles with fright!

I have a big fat cat,
He spends all day chasing a rat.
He's big and fat with lots of fur
When I stroke him I hear him purr.

I also have three fish
Nemo, Smimmer and Trish.
Smimmer is ill and floats upside down,
And Nemo has spots of yellow, blue and brown.

I have a big brown rabbit,
When I stick food through the cage he'll grab it.
Although he is very fat
He's thin compared to my big fat cat.

I also have a bat,
He flies away from the cat.
He's broken his left wing
And listens to the birds sing.

Isabel Lewis (10)
St Benedict Biscop Primary School, Wombourne

Autumn

A utumn colours speed across the hill-less ground
U nusual shiny brown conkers all shapes and sizes
T rees go bare or change colour to yellow, orange, bronze
U p goes the leaves swirling round and round
M ornings are getting mistier by the second
N ow more people are raking up the bumpy ground because
　　all the leaves are getting pushed down by the strong wind.

Megan Kiely (7)
St Benedict Biscop Primary School, Wombourne

School

I go to a school that has a big tree,
When I stand by it I feel the size of a flea.
I say hello every day when I get there,
But it doesn't really seem to care.

Lulu is my very best friend,
Notes to each other we always send.
Dot is the name of her pet dog,
But most of the time he sleeps like a log.

When we have sports I run and run,
We all enjoy it, it's so much fun.
We also give concerts in the hall,
Which gives pleasure to one and all.

This is my last year here,
I think I might shed a tear.
The day I leave will be so sad,
But I think the teachers will be glad.

I shall really miss Mr Stott,
He did teach me rather a lot.
He doesn't shout like some teachers do,
Only at the naughty few.

Then it's off to my new school
And having to learn each new rule.
Also there will be new teachers' names
And lots of different sports and games.

Ellie Thompson (10)
St Benedict Biscop Primary School, Wombourne

My Hamster

Her little eyes shimmer,
And her little teeth glimmer.
My hamster's nose twitches,
As the television switches.

She may be old, but she can be fast!
But in races, she'll be last.
In the exercise ball, she is quick,
But by her food bowl, that's where she sticks.

Her coat colour is peaches and cream,
But when she hurt her leg listen to her scream!
Nutmeg loves to eat my nan's meat pie,
She'll eat anything, I wonder why?

She loves to snooze on my lap
Because she's not into rap.
I play with her every day,
I just wonder what she has to say!

Nutmeg is very sweet,
And she loves chocolatey treats.
Nutmeg is my happy pet,
She has everything she can get.

Nutmeg loves the garden in the summer,
But she hates a novice drummer!
Her ears are soft and very fine.
I'm just glad Nutmeg's mine!

Lydia Meredith (11)
St Benedict Biscop Primary School, Wombourne

My Birthday

I wake up in the morning
I started the day yawning,
Oh yes it's my birthday yippee!
I can't believe I forgot I'm so silly.

I run downstairs as fast as I could
I would get some presents I know I would.
I stood there cheery and happy
Then my mom said, 'You're a cheery chappy.'

I went to the chair where they were sitting
I started to open them, it was exciting.
I thought I had finished opening them all
But something was sitting right by the wall.

I asked my mom, 'Is that for me?'
Mom said, 'Well that's the last present I can see.'
I don't have to go to school today
I can go out to play.

My birthday has been so cool
I might go to the pool,
I'm going to meet my friends there
And when we come out we will wash our hair.

My friends are so kind
They're always on my mind.
This has been the best birthday
I wish I could go on holiday.

Lucy Picken (11)
St Benedict Biscop Primary School, Wombourne

The Cricket Game

Today a cricket game is on, there goes a run
It's nearly lunchtime so I'll have a bun.
Michael Vaughan just took a good take,
In an hour's time I'll have a break.

The game is very close, look at the score
My friend today is such a bore.
As Andrew Flintoff starts to sprint
Somebody offers me a mint.

Soon somebody yells, *'Out!'*
And there's a crash on the roundabout.
Now the batsman's out with a stump
And the person behind me gives me a bump.

Andrew Straus gets a new bat
And I saw a man sitting on a mat.
This is now a brand new ball
Now somebody stands up who is very tall.

England get another wicket
Are we still playing cricket?
Now we get another four
Who has opened the door?

We get a big number six
Now I eat a king-size Twix.
The game is now over
The next game is in Dover.

Oliver Steel (10)
St Benedict Biscop Primary School, Wombourne

The Seaside Poem

There are a lot of people at the seaside
But you still have to keep an eye on the tide.
There are some salty smelly smells
And there are plenty of colourful shells.

Then the sea
Is very clean.
Have a picnic on the sand
Listen to your favourite band.

Have a fish on your dish
Find a well and make a wish.
Take in the fresh air
If you want a snack have a pear.

Look at a boat
Look at it float
Away from the rocks
Near the docks.

Some of the waves
Go in underwater caves.
You might go fishing with a rod and hook
You might sit down and read a book.

Enjoy the last of the sun
Because the day is done.
If you've worn suncream you will not frown
If you did not you will be brown.

Christopher Rogers (10)
St Benedict Biscop Primary School, Wombourne

Things I Like

I like pop
And I also like rock.
My favourite is rap
And I listen to it wearing a cap.

I like magnificent things
I like diamonds and rings.
I really love gold
But I really hate mould.

I like cuddly toys
But I hate most boys.
I like my brothers
But no others.

I quite like school
And the teachers rule.
I don't like tests
But I always try to do my best.

I really like money
But not honey.
I've got a dog
That snores like a hog.

I like to smile
I've smiled for a while.
I like TV
But best of all I like me.

Olivia Collier (10)
St Benedict Biscop Primary School, Wombourne

Monster

There's a monster somewhere
But I don't know where.
I think it's in the shed
Where I dare not go.

'Monster, monster under the stairs!'

I saw it the other day once or twice
With a couple of dead mice.
It made me shudder,
So I ran to my mother.

'Monster, monster under the stairs!'

It's got red eyes
Like blackberry pies
A head like rocks
And a neck like blocks
With blue and yellow spots
Feet like leaves
With added reeds.

'Monster, monster under the stairs!'

Emily Howe (10)
St Benedict Biscop Primary School, Wombourne

Autumn

The wind is blowing through trees
Swishing in my ear,
The leaves were dancing on the stage
Like ballet dancers gracefully
When the horse gallops through the leaves
Making sounds as if I were eating crisps
When I am asleep the wind tangles my hair
The wind is like the alarm clock
That wakes me up early in the morning
I love the autumn
To see all the children playing in the leaves.

Ninette Moseley-Harris (10)
St Benedict Biscop Primary School, Wombourne

Fire

When you first light a fire the flames start to dance,
The wood starts to turn black at the same speed you can ride a bike.
The sap starts to spit in your face
And when you get smoke in your eyes it makes you cry tears of pain.
When you first feel the heat hit your face you think you're in an oven.
Because it's so hot, you cannot believe it.
When you blow into the ashes they fly into your face
Now the fire is out the show is over,
It is waiting to be cleaned and lit again.

Adam Fitzgerald (10)
St Benedict Biscop Primary School, Wombourne

The Storm

The storm raged towards the city like an angry bull.
Its fingers destroyed anything in its path
Leaving a trail of scattered debris behind it.
But still it charged as fast as possible.
And suddenly it hit the city with a mighty clap of thunder.
It thrashed the city till there was nothing left but rubble.
The storm gave one last bolt of lightning,
The city shuddered with fear
But with one last grumble the storm changed for the next city.

Kyle Parkes (10)
St Benedict Biscop Primary School, Wombourne

There Was A Small Cuddly Hamster

There was a small, cuddly hamster
Who also was a very good dancer.
He danced all day
In every which way
That small and cuddly hamster.

Nicole Stoddart (10)
St Benedict Biscop Primary School, Wombourne

A Delicious Cake

A lovely little cake
With a big chocolate flake.
If it had double cream
It would be my dream.

The icing was gooey
But the sweets were ever so chewy.
The cake was yummy
And it rumbled in my tummy.

We mixed it in a bowl
And made it into a roll.
I put it in the oven
And it smelt like Heaven.

Me and my chef used to bake it
And I used to take it.
But it was so nice
People used to give me a slice!

I put in a sweet
It was the kids' treat.
On top I put candy sticks
And now it's a mix.

In it I put chocolate fudge
Now it's turned into sludge.
So eat and eat
And I'll beat.

Katie Grainger (10)
St Benedict Biscop Primary School, Wombourne

Animals

I have a big black cat
Who is very, very fat.
When he goes out at night
He gives the birds a fright!

My friend Emma has a dog
Which likes to sit on a log.
He barks all the time
And pulls down the washing line!

I once saw a fish
Who was washing on a dish.
He was orange and violet and yellow and blue
And purple and green, he was very new.

I've been riding on a horse
And I've seen it doing a course.
It could do very high jumps
But wasn't very good on the bumps.

I saw a dolphin doing a flip
So I thought I might take a dip.
When I was swimming in the water
I saw my mom with her daughter.

Bo Peep crying because she'd lost her sheep
But then she found then all in a heap.
When the sheep were eating grass
A tractor whizzed right past.

Kaitlin Cole (10)
St Benedict Biscop Primary School, Wombourne

Animal Mayhem

There was a cat
He sat on a mat,
When I stroked its long fur
He purred.

There was a dog
He jumped like a frog,
But he might,
You never know, he may bite.

There was an owl
If you woke him he would scowl
He goes, 'Hoot, hoot'
If he sees a hunter he says, 'Please don't shoot!'

There was a sheep
And he went bleep
And then he went to sleep
In a big heap.

There was a rat
He sat on a mat,
And he wore a hat
That was flat.

There was a mouse
Who lived in my house
Who ate cheese
And who is called Louise.

Oliver Hill (10)
St Benedict Biscop Primary School, Wombourne

My Dad When He Was A Lad

I have a wicked dad
Who always talks about when he was a lad.
He loved Pukka Pies
And when he had one he wore a tie.

He had a brother called Tom
Who had a cuddly bear called Dom.
Tom loved his food especially chips
When he ate a juicy apple he ate the pips.

He had a dad called John
Who always played with younger Tom.
His dad hates gum he thinks it's gross
That's what he hates most.

He has a mom called Pam
Who always has lovely jam!
She absolutely hates fast cars
But she adores empty jars.

My dad had a dog
He always took it out for a jog.
The dog hates cats
Especially Postman Pat's!

Last of all he has a cat
His cat is very fat.
His cat loves fish
He has it on a colourful dish.

Liam Murphy-Parnwell (10)
St Benedict Biscop Primary School, Wombourne

Walking The Dog

There is a very big dog
Who sleeps as still as a log
And if you stroke its fur,
It will always purr.

If you throw a stick
He will retrieve it very quick.
He'll jump in the stream and get wet
That's my pet.

You have to keep him on a lead
Because he is a very rare breed.
And he will see a bone
He will chase it all alone!

He's a very fit dog
Who jumps higher than a frog.
If he looks as if he is going to bite
He won't, he'll just fight.

He won't go out at night
Because normally he has a big fright.
And when it is dark
He will always bark.

There's this bloke
Every time he walks past he has to have a stroke
And when we come back we give him something meaty
Which we call a 'treaty.'

John Howell (10)
St Benedict Biscop Primary School, Wombourne

Fear

Fingers of fear wrap themselves around my throat,
Grasping my voice box so tightly I am speechless.
I feel a million shivers creeping down my spine.
I dive down under my bed, terrified.
It's coming, it's got me, I panic,
My brain tells me,
Stay here,
Stay here,
Don't move.
So I lie there,
Motionless,
Speechless,
Breathless.

Olivia Churchill (10)
St Benedict Biscop Primary School, Wombourne

Autumn

A utumn is coming, hooray, hooray!
U sually animals are hibernating, squirrels and hedgehogs.
T oo many bronze leaves settling on the wet soggy lawn.
U nusual smells are drifting across your face and bare trees
                                  are leaning over your head.
M igrating is the thing that birds do every autumn by flying
                                  from this country to another.
N o more scorching hot weather anymore!

Jazzmin Jowett (7)
St Benedict Biscop Primary School, Wombourne

Autumn

A utumn is coming,
U sually the nights get colder,
T he leaves are changing into different colours,
U p in the tall trees squirrels are gathering their nuts,
M ornings are getting mistier,
N uts are getting buried by the squirrels.

Rebecca Roberts (7)
St Benedict Biscop Primary School, Wombourne

Autumn

A ll the golden leaves in autumn fall down from the tall trees.
U sually in autumn the shiny conkers break out of the spiky shells.
T he leaves are gold, yellow, red, orange and bronze.
U p in the trees there are not a lot of golden leaves left.
M ornings are getting shorter, mistier and damper.
N uts are being brought in by squirrels.

Lauren Tarrant (7)
St Benedict Biscop Primary School, Wombourne

Autumn

A utumn leaves golden, yellow and bronze falling off the bare trees
U sually children kick leaves with a crunchy sound
T he birds migrating to warmer countries
U sing a rake to rake up the leaves
M ornings are misty and foggy and dull
N ights are longer, days are shorter.

Gemma Sutton (7)
St Benedict Biscop Primary School, Wombourne

Autumn

A utumn leaves falling from the trees in all different colours
red, orange, yellow
U nusual sounds on Hallowe'en
T winkling wet cobwebs in the bare bushes
U sually there are more robins in the frosted leaves
M igrating birds going somewhere warmer
N ipping winds in the air.

Natasha Jones (7)
St Benedict Biscop Primary School, Wombourne

Autumn

A nimals start to hibernate,
U p in the brown trees the leaves fall slowly down
T winkling webs shine in the shiny sun
U nder the dark brown trees are shiny glowing conkers
M any birds are migrating
N oisy squirrels are after green tasty nuts.

Lucas Chivers (7)
St Benedict Biscop Primary School, Wombourne

Autumn

A ll the golden yellow leaves fall off the tall trees
U p in the swaying trees the red squirrels collect small nuts
T he animals are getting ready to hibernate in the spring
U p in the trees the grey squirrels are making a nest
M isty weather starts to come
N ights start to get dark and gloomy.

Nicholas Poulton (7)
St Benedict Biscop Primary School, Wombourne

Autumn

A ll soft leaves are falling, colours are red, yellow and gold
U p-crawling spiders make sticky cobwebs everywhere
T ackling the blowing wind to hibernate
U gly smacking weather just gets me in a bad temper
M aking the spiky conkers more prickly
N ice, friendly robins or hairy squirrels are gathering enormous nuts.

Noel Howell (7)
St Benedict Biscop Primary School, Wombourne

Autumn

A utumn is here, it's a happy day today
U sually conkers falling down and cracking their prickly spiky shells
T rees dropping red, yellow, green, gold elegant flakes
U nder children's feet leaves crackling as they jump on them
M ist blocking the windows annoying parents going to work
N uts on the ground for squirrels to eat.

Frances Hopson (7)
St Benedict Biscop Primary School, Wombourne

Autumn

A utumn is the time for animals to hibernate
U p in the trees there are green spiky conkers
T he mornings are misty and cold
U p in the trees, leaves are ready to fall
M ore birds leave England to migrate
N ight-time is long.

Callum Cox (7)
St Benedict Biscop Primary School, Wombourne

Tiger, Tiger

(Inspired by 'The Tyger' by William Blake)

Tiger, tiger burning bright
Won't you share us your roars tonight.
Tiptoeing in the jungle night
So say to him, 'Sleep tight.'

When he wakes up at dawn
He looks for his food.
He will scratch his back on a tree
Like a cool dude.

In the jungle he is prowling around
He is looking, looking.
Nowhere to be found
You will see him in the trees ducking, ducking.

Charlotte Green (9)
St Benedict Biscop Primary School, Wombourne

My Dad

My dad is a policeman
He wears a big black hat
He carries silver handcuffs
And a metal bat!

He drives in a nee naa
Like Starsky and Hutch
He loves catching robbers
I love my dad so much.

Jack Lowe (7)
St Benedict Biscop Primary School, Wombourne

Autumn

A utumn is the time when animals start to hibernate
U p in the cold shivery trees all the squirrels start to collect shiny nuts
T he spiky shells start to fall off the shivering trees
U nder the trees the coloured leaves like red, brown,
orange, gold, yellow, bronze
M y dad saw a hedgehog getting ready for the winter
when he was gardening
N oisy birds flying and playing while they are migrating.

Jackson Mulvihill (7)
St Benedict Biscop Primary School, Wombourne

Autumn

A ll the leaves are falling off the trees onto the floor
U p in the big blue sky it is getting darker and colder
T he blue sky is getting misty and damp
U sually people have things to make them warm in autumn
M ornings are getting misty as it gets to autumn
N ights are getting darker as it comes to night-time in autumn.

James Harris (7)
St Benedict Biscop Primary School, Wombourne

Autumn

A utumn is a time when animals hibernate
U sually animals, like squirrels, find food for the winter
T he birds fly to a warmer country in the winter
U sually animals try to find homes to hibernate in the winter
M isty, colder, foggy mornings are arriving
N ights are getting darker.

Keeley Green (7)
St Benedict Biscop Primary School, Wombourne

My Dogs

I have two little dogs
They are very clever clogs.
They play with balls
And come when they are called.

Cassie is quite hairy
And Jakie is quite scary.
He bit me on the thigh
But I didn't cry.

Kelly Warrington (8)
St Benedict Biscop Primary School, Wombourne

Chocolate

Chocolate, chocolate
I love chocolate
Imagine if chocolate was everywhere
Chocolate for breakfast
Chocolate for tea
Oh what glee
Chocolate makes the world go round
What a lovely sound.

Daniel Bonser (8)
St Benedict Biscop Primary School, Wombourne

Matt's Cat

There once was a man called Matt
He was dreadfully scared of his cat
The cat had big claws
And tiny jaws
And was as small as Matt's mat.

Matthew Allsebrook (9)
St Benedict Biscop Primary School, Wombourne

Autumn

Autumn is coming.
Autumn is when all the animals start to hibernate.
Under the hedges you can see little sparkly cobwebs
Because the rain has been on the cobwebs.
The trees are bare because all the leaves, nuts and conkers
have fallen.
The conkers break out of their bright, prickly, spiky, green shells
on the trees.
Bare trees there are lots of creatures underneath.
Mainly you see lots of creatures in the bright green bushes.
No more seeing creatures in the winter.

Matthew Lewis (7)
St Benedict Biscop Primary School, Wombourne

Autumn

A utumn is when the leaves start to fall
U p in the trees the conkers are falling down
T he leaves are changing colour
U p in the trees there are robins singing
M ore birds are migrating to a different country
N ight-time gets darker earlier and the mornings are cold and foggy.

Joe Shotton (7)
St Benedict Biscop Primary School, Wombourne

Autumn

A utumn, the wintry time of year is here
U sual golden, red leaves drifting down
T he coming excitement of Hallowe'en late October
U sual frosty surprise
M ost people start having hot water bottles
N ow you know what autumn's about, if I were you,
you'd better watch out!

Lucia Greenwood (7)
St Benedict Biscop Primary School, Wombourne

Autumn

A utumn is coming!

U nderground animals hibernating, squirrels with nuts

T he birds migrating, hungry red robins searching for red berries

U sually the brown trees are bare, golden and red leaves
                                    fall on the ground

M isty, cold, damp mornings, car windows steamed up

N o more shiny round conkers on the ground,
            people have taken them, only the green, spiky cases left.

Samuel Cartwright (8)
St Benedict Biscop Primary School, Wombourne

Autumn

A ll different coloured shiny leaves falling off the bare brown trees

U nhappy now the bright sun has gone

T rying hard to keep snug and warm

U nluckily now we can't sunbathe!

M ums rushing to get ready for Christmas

N ights get longer and darker.

Lucy Steel (7)
St Benedict Biscop Primary School, Wombourne

Autumn

A ll around are berries on the trees

U p in the trees squirrels gather nuts

T he shiny brown conkers in a spiky shell

U p on the wall you can see a cobweb from a spider

M isty mornings appear after the night

N ow the animals start to hibernate.

Ryan Preece (7)
St Benedict Biscop Primary School, Wombourne

Friends

Friends are here to help you through
All the things that trouble you.
When you're getting bullied it gets you down
Friends are here to cheer you up, don't frown.

They help you study when you're stuck
When you enter a test they wish you luck.
When you fall and hurt your knee
They will patch it up and I'll smile with glee.

Friends are great to look after you
Do you like them? I do!
But remember it's not just you
They also need help too!

But most people have one of these
They're called best friends, they never tease.
They are a bit like your sister with the same hobbies
Their favourite food is pizza and they love ice lollies.

My friends are the best thing that happened to me
When we're out I'm sad to go in for tea.
We go round in a group, the chip shop, we meet there
And we're all so funny when we play truth or dare!

Harriet Kommant (10)
St Benedict Biscop Primary School, Wombourne

Crazy Clock

There was a young lady from Bong,
Who had a clock that went dong,
It drove her mad
And she was so sad
That she smashed the clock until it went wrong.

Charlotte Lander (9)
St Benedict Biscop Primary School, Wombourne

Famous Cars

Cars, cars, where shall I start, if children want to drive
They start with a go-kart,
There's the Dukes of Hazzard General Lee
You could start it if you ever found the key!

The most famous Batmobile with the Bat logo on the wheel
The Starsky and Hutch, Ford Grand Torino,
When you start it you just have to shout, 'Let's go!'

If you have a Ford Mustang
You just have to show your gang!
The Reliant Robin from 'Only Fools and Horses'
They are fools but not horses.

Stallion, oh stallion, if you drive one you don't have to be Italian
The Dodge Viper it makes the drivers hyper!

Aston Martin V12 Vanquish
In 'Die Another Day' like a shot it can vanish!
You might be keen to go 'Back To The Future'
In the Deloren Time Machine!

Bond thought it was a dream,
So drive the Sunbeam
The '2 Fast, 2 Furious' movie car
Is a Nissan Skyline GTR!

James Crowther (10)
St Benedict Biscop Primary School, Wombourne

Autumn

A utumn is coming
U p high then on the floor
T all trees dropping leaves down on the floor
U sually conkers come out of their brown or green prickly cases
M ammals start to hibernate under the cosy layer of leaves
N uts are being hidden by cheeky squirrels in the ground.

Jack Tomlinson (7)
St Benedict Biscop Primary School, Wombourne

Chocolate Allsorts

Chocolates can be really creamy,
They also sound so badly dreamy.
Some chocolates are rather crunchy,
Others are deliciously munchy.

You can buy nuts,
That look like soot.
Some can be fruity,
And shaped like a bootie.

Willy Wonka the greatest chocolatier,
Cadbury's can make the giant chocolate ear,
Galaxy gets the best design,
Golden lagging way behind.

Celebrations are what you eat,
They're so pleasurable they give you a tingle in your feet.
Miniature Heroes save starvation,
And make you on time for the station.

They can be really bubbly,
They are supposed to be so chocolatey
You can eat them your own way,
As long as you eat them off a tray.

You can't get chocolate that's cheesy,
And you will get very wheezy
Orange chocolate was invented,
But had to be dented!

Emma Dallimore (10)
St Benedict Biscop Primary School, Wombourne

The Old Man From Cleves

There was an old man from Cleves,
Who was stung by wasps and bees,
It caused him pain,
He did complain!
The poor old man from Cleves.

Alessandro Gibson (9)
St Benedict Biscop Primary School, Wombourne

Autumn

A utumn leaves start to fall slowly off the brown trees
   what nice colours they are, gold, yellow, orange and bronze
U h no, it's getting dark so early
T rees are so bare, what brown branches they have
U nder the ground hedgehogs in their prickly ball are hibernating
M isty mornings can't see where you're going
N asty spider webs in the bushes, make sure the spider
                                        doesn't get you!

Harry Greensill (7)
St Benedict Biscop Primary School, Wombourne

Autumn

A utumn is coming and squirrels are climbing
U p the tall trees collecting all the small nuts
T he hedgehogs are curling up in a spiky ball just like conkers
U sually green leaves turn red and orange
M any big people gather conkers of all shapes and sizes
                                        ready for a great battle
N   one enters the Haunted House where a Hallowe'en
                                        surprise is waiting.

Joseph Atton (7)
St Benedict Biscop Primary School, Wombourne

Autumn

A utumn is coming
U nder the bushes fall big brown shiny conkers in the green shells.
T rees are losing their leaves and all the different colours are falling
U nfortunately the nights are getting longer
M y house is filled with cobwebs of spiders
N ever go outside without a coat because you can catch a cold.

Put your coat on it will be a lot better so people can go out.

Ben Davis-Moore (8)
St Benedict Biscop Primary School, Wombourne

Shark

There was a hungry old shark,
Who truly loved to eat bark.
He couldn't find any in the sea,
So he tried to eat fish
But couldn't manage it.
So he tried to drink the sea.

Daniel Roberts (9)
St Benedict Biscop Primary School, Wombourne

Our Playground

In the playground you will see
Children playing happily
In the playground you will find
Boys shooting hoops and girls running loops.
Frisbees are flying through the air
Duck! Watch out! They might mess up your hair
Skipping ropes are swinging high,
The colourful parachute in the sky.
The football pitch, bat and ball,
They are all waiting for the call
Our playground is fun, there's lots to do.
Our playground is safe, it's interesting too.
We should be kind and we should share.
Be nice to one another and care.

Natarleya Drummond (9)
St Catherine of Siena RC Primary School, Birmingham

One Hundred Years From Now!

One hundred years from now
It will not matter
What kind of car I drive
Or
What kind of house I live in
Or
How much money is in my bank
Or
What my clothes look like,
But the world may be a better place because
I was important in the life of a child.

Laura Payne (9)
St Catherine of Siena RC Primary School, Birmingham

Mum's Love

Mum you mean the world to me,
In everything you do,
So I have written this special poem especially for you,
You take care of me in the best of ways,
Giving me some of the best days,
I love you, Mum, you know it's true
And I know I love you with my whole heart too
I really want to thank you, Mum
For all the things you do
And I'd like to say above all else, Mum, thanks for being you.

Sarah-Jane Taylor (10)
St Catherine of Siena RC Primary School, Birmingham

The Haunted House

People say the witch lives there.
With her red sparkling eyes and long grey hair.
They say she has a cauldron pot,
Which children seem to visit a lot.

In there she lives the children shout
She never ever seems to come out.

She will always carry her spell book
Or zap you away in her huge handy truck.
The howling always makes you scream
But if she hears you she'll give you bad dreams.

'In there she lives,' the children shout
She never ever seems to come out.

Now I'm off to go to my home
If you need me give me a phone
For the haunted house will give you bad dreams.
You will now hear and see unwanted things.
Goodnight!

Joanna Tomlin (11)
St James' CE Primary School, Handsworth

School

School is a place to work and play,
And be on your best behaviour all day.
If you want to talk do it in the playground,
But when you're in class don't make a sound
When you go swimming or do PE,
It's important to warm up properly
Different subjects are science or RE.
But my favourite ones are art and DT.
Some people are good and some are bad,
Some make me happy and some make me mad.
At school there are many things to see,
Because school is a great place for everyone to be!

Keilah Chambers (9)
St James' CE Primary School, Handsworth

I Rule School!

School is cool,
Because I rule,
Over all the teachers,
And even the head.

When it comes to playtime
I'm the next Miss Eve,
Because I make all the teachers,
Pick up all the leaves.

Dinner times, dinner times they just get better,
Oh, how I wish they were less wetter,
So we could go outside to play,
And rule the school another day.

Lessons, lessons I haven't decided about them yet,
The teachers wish we had them, I bet,
But anyway it's so cool,
When I rule school!

Sophie Smith (11)
St James' CE Primary School, Handsworth

Harvest

I can hear people go
Chatter, chatter, chatter,
Harvest time is here.
I can hear the leaves go
Crunch, crunch, crunch.
I can hear people eat vegetables
Munch, munch, munch.

Mariyam Abid (9)
St James' CE Primary School, Handsworth

Harvest Time Once Again

All the fruits ripen in the sun
Different types of food coming in a tonne.

We share out the food and grain
They've all grown thanks to the rain.

Golden corn, beanstalks
The farmer watches out for crows as he walks.

We grind grain to make flour
Eating healthy food gives us power.

Different foods, for different species or things
Birds sit in the tree, eat worms and sing.

Cabbages are healthy and green
Broccoli with saucy beans.

Mash potato with sweetcorn
Harvest is when food is born.

Harvest time has come so let's celebrate!
Yum-yum!

Safina Mughal (10)
St James' CE Primary School, Handsworth

My Best Friend

He talked with me before it all began.
He walked with me and showed me that I can.
He holds me up each time I fall,
And listens to me every time I call.
He rescues me when I lose my way,
And guides me safely from evil prey,
He wipes away my tears when I'm feeling sad,
God's the greatest friend that I've ever had.

Michael Mitchell (7)
St James' CE Primary School, Handsworth

Land Of Sweet Surprises

Far away and yet among us
Lies a country all have seen,
Cloudless skies and golden woodlands,
Silver waters, meadows green
And the voice of the city,
And sounds of toil and strife.

Never reach that lovely country
Never spoil its happy life
For the land of sweet surprise
Is the children's world of joy.

Shantelle Notice (9)
St James' CE Primary School, Handsworth

The Chicks

Chicks are here,
Chicks are there,
Chicks are hatching everywhere!
Poking out their tiny beaks,
They open wide calling, *'Cheep! Cheep!'*

So, is this a special day,
When all the chicks come out to play?
Yes, it is hip hip hooray!
At last, it's happy hatching day.

Nasir Mahdi
St James' CE Primary School, Handsworth

The World

The world is beautiful
The grass is green
The sky is like a white cream
Some trees are tall
The leaves are small
Some animals are elegant
And humans are elegant
Houses let us live
Like we have lots to give
So that's our world and how we live
The world is beautiful.

Larissa Carr (10)
St James' CE Primary School, Handsworth

Autumn's Here

Autumn is here,
Christmas is near.

The spirits are lighted,
I am so excited.

The leaves are falling down,
They make a rustling sound.

The birds are singing,
It's so cold the wasps are not stinging.

The trees are blowing side to side,
The animals are all going to hide.

Kirandeep Sandhu (10)
St James' CE Primary School, Handsworth

My Brother

My brother is a baby
He is really cute (maybe).
His name is Shaquille,
He eats a lot of meals.
Shaquille smiles a lot,
Even when he is in his cot.
Shaquille has got straight hair,
And I don't think it is fair.
I love him,
He loves me,
We are happy in a family.

Ayannah Manning (10)
St James' CE Primary School, Handsworth

Mr Darkness

Darkness creeps over the world
Like an unexpected visitor,
Spreading everywhere filling the sky
In every corner like paint
Being painted onto the sky,
We sleep while the visitor is still here,
And when we wake up
Mr Darkness slowly puts on his hat and coat
And fades away.

Arundeep Bains (10)
St James' CE Primary School, Handsworth

All About Parents

Dad
Strong yet gentle,
Firm but fair,
Good times and bad,
You're always there.
Like the warming sun
In the morning skies
We live in the love
That shines in your eyes.

Mum
A heart that's full of gentleness.
And love beyond compare,
Hands that smooth and comfort,
When the hurt is hard to bear.
A mum's combination of gifts we all possess,
She uses them to brighten life and spread real happiness.

Aleesha Hussain (10)
St James' CE Primary School, Handsworth

Skeleton Parade

The skeletons are out tonight,
They march about the street
With bony bodies, bony heads
And bony hands and feet.

Bony, bony, bony bones
With nothing in-between
Up and down and all around
They march on Hallowe'en.

Nazish Haider (10)
St James' CE Primary School, Handsworth

The Hill

The hill in the distance so glum and so dark
As I walk closer I feel a spark.
The sadness and grief fills my heart
Every section of every part.
As I walk closer I hear a story
Of a man who's been robbed of his glory.
I can hear screams and a cry
The voice of whom was pitched so high.
You can imagine what he went through
It's the saddest story one has ever known.
At the top of the hill his body lay
As his soul remembers and remembers that day.

Jaspreet Bhurjee (11)
St James' CE Primary School, Handsworth

My Family

My family are the Notemans and the Francisis.
They are always late for everything.
I have fourteen cousins
And most of them are younger than me.
I am the oldest granddaughter of the Notemans
And I'm proud of it.
That means that at Christmas I have a lot of presents to buy.
My aunty is a Muslim
So I can learn about another religion.
As well as Christianity.
I love my family.

Ebony Francis (10)
St James' CE Primary School, Handsworth

Lucy's School

Lucy's school was a horrific place,
It always led to a disgrace!
The teachers gave each other a curse!
The head teacher was even worse!
The headmistress was really fat,
Her size was as small as a rat!
Her friends looked like some ugly witches!
They called themselves Mrs Twitches.
Miss Jackson her music teacher,
Was a hilarious creature!
Last but not least Mrs Fadeey
Was her crazy dinner lady!
Yes, Lucy's school was a horrific place,
It always led to disgrace!

Charnjeev Kaur (10)
St James' CE Primary School, Handsworth

Buried Treasure

I went on a treasure hunt
To see what I could find.
Maybe it is in front of the tree
Maybe it's behind.
You never know where it is
Wait until it's found.
Look around
Hear and listen to the sound.
So I went to get my dog
And I said, *'Dig, dig, dig!'*
When we got the treasure it was big.
It was a dog bone my dog had dug.
So then we turned around and saw a bug.

Michael Fearon (9)
St James' CE Primary School, Handsworth

The Solar System

Mercury is as hot
As a noodle pot.
Venus is bright
Especially at night.
I live on Earth
The place of my birth.
Mars is full of CO_2
I wonder if it has a loo.
Jupiter has a spot
Almost like a dot.
Saturn has rings of rocks and dust
I wonder if you will find any rust.
Uranus is pale blue
I'd like to see that too.
Neptune's cold
I wonder if anyone has been told.
Pluto's moon is called Charan
And my name is Aran.

Aran Singh (9)
St James' CE Primary School, Handsworth

Fireworks

Fireworks, fireworks, standing by!
Blowing up in the sky!
Just like roses opening!
My beautiful flowers in the sky!

Amandeep Nijjar (8)
St James' CE Primary School, Handsworth

Life In School

Life in school is quite cool,
In fact I think it's very good.

Science, math and ICT are the best,
Far more better than the rest.

My life with my teachers is just ace,
Because they want to give a better working pace.

Deputy, Head and my class teacher are very funny and jolly,
But beware they can get angry when you get sweets 'n' lollies.

Life with my friends is just great,
How I met them must be fate.

Life out of school is so good,
Museum, park or woodland all information is understood.

My life throughout school is a dream,
All the teachers make a great team.

Mohammed Chowdury (10)
St James' CE Primary School, Handsworth

Friends

Friends are kind,
But hard to find.
Friends are there,
When you're at the fair.
Friends are nice,
But they don't like mice
Friends are sweet,
And like nice treats.
Friends are caring
When you are crying
Friends are sad,
When you feel bad.
Friends are kind,
But hard to find.

Anisha Jassal (10)
St James' CE Primary School, Handsworth

Rabbit!

My *rabbit, rabbit, rabbit*
Has a very naughty *habbit, habbit, habbit*
Of scratching, nibbling and twitching his nose
Jumping in the air is how he likes to pose!
Drinking water *non-stop, non-stop*
Eating, eating until he will *pop, pop, pop*
His name is *Binker, Binker, Binker*
Oh, what a *tinker, tinker, tinker!*
But still I love him so
I'm sure you all know!

Abigail Hawthorne (10)
St Mary's RC Primary School, Brierley Hill

Joe I Love Him So

Joe, Joe I love him so
His little tail hanging low
Snow-white paws, which twinkle so glorious in the sun.
Oh my little *cat, cat, cat*
Chasing that *rat, rat, rat*
When I am sad I hear your purring
It soothes my heart of sorrow
As I give you a cuddle
You bow your head and give me a snuggle.

Georgia Stevens (10)
St Mary's RC Primary School, Brierley Hill

Cute Little Pup!

Mummy bought me a cute little pup
She said she thought it would shut me up
He's black and white, with eyes so bright
A cold wet nose and muddy paws
Happily chewing on my best pink draws
'Don't let him do that,' said Mum with a frown
Oh he's definitely funny, just like a clown
He makes me laugh when I give him a bath
The way he walks and wags his tail
Always the first to get to the mail
Toby's his name and funny by nature
That's my poem to give the taycher.

Chloe Broadbent (10)
St Mary's RC Primary School, Brierley Hill

The Pond

Silver sparkles gleam and shine,
Reflections in the dazzling sun,
Green-back croakers jump about,
Among the reeds they have great fun!

Tiny tadpoles twist and turn,
In the sky-blue water twirling,
While overhead the swallows fly,
And the fluffy clouds are swirling.

Ruth Griffin (10)
St Mary's RC Primary School, Brierley Hill

Natalie

Sometimes I hit her
Sometimes I hate her
But I will always love her
We drive each other round the bend
But still we're the best of friends.
Every night when I go to bed
I never forget to kiss her
After all, oh after all, she'll always be my sister.

Bethanie Hancox (10)
St Mary's RC Primary School, Brierley Hill

Monsters

Hairy, scary
Please be wary
Monsters can be quite contrary
Highly willing
Acting slyly
Don't believe them when they're smiley.
Better to follow a hunch
Than end up in a monster's lunch.

Zarrah Belgian (10)
St Mary's RC Primary School, Brierley Hill

Wind Poem

Wind whistling through, through the air it rages
It lashes out at trees
Nothing can stop it
Destroying everything in its way.

Wind tearing through paper bags
It pounces in and out
No one is about no one dares
Destruction everywhere.

Wind, when will it stop?
It will silently approach
No one will hear as it rips apart its prey
Diminished in seconds.

As it grows old
It starts to retire
Then falls down *dead!*

Nick Jones (10)
Sharmans Cross Junior School

The Day Of The Storm

The clouds approach,
Like a hungry lion,
Roaring, growling
Throwing bolts of light,
At any random person
Frightening people with louder roars and its red eyes,
Attacking poachers for their evil doings,
Scared of no one
Roaring louder, taking a shower urges on more . . .

People so scared of dying
Many friends, people dying
Its job is done,
Walks away laughing.

Luke Lindsey (10)
Sharmans Cross Junior School

Tornado

He awakes silently from his sleep
His devilish eyes shine,
Searching over town,
Looking for his prey.

Bang!
He finds it,
He roars furiously into the air,
Causing chaos,
He pounces on the cursed town.

With his claws he rips bushes,
Trees fall down as he shouts angrily,
Crash, smash, boom,
Bricks and tiles hit the ground.

His red eyes search the disaster,
For another victim,
He sets his eyes on a single house,
Still clinging to the Earth.

He blows,
But nothing happens to the house,
So with a flick of his tail,
He returns to his den.

Taran Basi (10)
Sharmans Cross Junior School

Untitled

Tumbling down the rocky mountain
Hidden beneath the droopy waves
Getting deeper as it goes along
Disturbing creatures on its way
Getting faster and faster as it passes by
Tumbling and tumbling till it reaches the sea
Until it reaches a river in the world
And starts all over again.

Laura Lister & Aimee Thomas (9)
Sharmans Cross Junior School

The Cracking Lightning And Booming Thunder

Slowly, a creature lurks in the mist,
Silently he walks searching for a victim.
Suddenly the mist starts to move,
The tiger is revealed and it ducks down low.
It pounces, clawing at the victim,
Blood drips down, millions of droplets at a time.

Like thousands of animals at a time,
Feel the rain dripping from above,
Crack! Hear the lightning from above.
Everything starts to get scared.
Boom! They start stamping on the ground,
Hoping for a way to get out.

Like a bird of prey looking down from the sky,
It sees a rampage of animals charging.
It waits for the perfect moment and then,
Crack! It swoops down with tremendous speed,
Burning everything it touches.
Now it's grabbed its animal, it fades away.

Jake Thomas (10)
Sharmans Cross Junior School

The Wild Snowstorm

The cloud silently emerging from the distance
Gliding across the land
Spreading feathers onto the ground
Forming a blanket of fur
People running outside to play
Moving swiftly along the sky
Grabbing at its prey
Spreading the last bundle of feathers
Upon the freezing earth
Then gliding swiftly away.

Jessica Smith (10)
Sharmans Cross Junior School

The Tornado Has Struck

It's coming!
Getting closer by the minute, we are all going to die
Coiling a web around this tiny world

It's coming!
Slowly but noisily it's tapping to us now
Turning and twirling, spinning and rotating and wrapping

It's here!
Stretching out its thin and tiny arms and legs
It's snapping houses and throwing them in the sky

It's here!
Blowing a fresh windy blow to make our bodies shiver
Tapping legs and spinning a web

It's gone!
To find another place to hide
It's destroyed our lives and broken our hearts once more

It's gone!
Luckily it's gone, to spin another web
Where has it gone now? Nobody knows.

Holly Cookson (10)
Sharmans Cross Junior School

Waterfall

Icy blue waterfall tumbles down
The powerful water crashes on rocks
Mist hangs in the air.

Now the river flows fast
Rushing restlessly past stones
Joining bigger rivers.

Strong rapids getting faster, faster
Finally joining the sea
Its journey ends.

Emma Taylor & Carolyne Lloyd (10)
Sharmans Cross Junior School

The Destroyer

The clouds quickly darken

The wind picks up rushing
Their big feet pounding towards the enemy.
Suddenly there comes a crash and a bang.

Lightning and thunder crash off the roof of their enemy's head
The hurricane starts to build up,
Waking from last year full of energy.
Lightning bashes down an electricity post
And their enemy loses power.
The stampede starts pawing the ground
Taking gravel and house with them.
Whirling dust and tiles round in the air.

The hurricane finally stops and suddenly suddenly drops dead
But everywhere flooded.
Victims of the hurricane stop and cry
Their homes destroyed from the traumatised storm.

Everybody finally gets over the storm.
Overjoyed to get back their lives.

Laura Bowen (10)
Sharmans Cross Junior School

Waterfall

W hirling through the rough rocks
A massive wave crashes down.
T orrential waves splashing on rapid rocks.
E merging water splashing everywhere.
R ushing down rapid rocks
F urious waterfall running rapidly.
A ngry waves splash down to kill.
L arge waves crash down to earth.
L onely waves run along.

Kerry Holmes & Lucie-Anne Fowkes (9)
Sharmans Cross Junior School

Storm

Noiselessly he descends on his prey,
His frightening, sooty face looms over the city,
He grins and roars,
The rain pelts down.

His silvery cutting claw scratches,
Sending flashes of golden lightning down,
Its humongous paws clap together
Making cracking, crashing sounds.

He leaps and then pounces,
Down fall the trees,
He purrs, the wind whistles,
His distant cousins, the wolves howl,
He's had enough, he charges and leaves the city.
House battered, lives shattered.

Amy Richards (11)
Sharmans Cross Junior School

Rivers

Trickling down the mountains
Swirling round the rocks
Getting faster and faster
No one knows when it stops
Getting wider and wider
Does it end at the sea?

People sailing down the river
Boats chugging by
No one knows when to stop
Getting wider and wider
Will they end at the sea?

Michael Finch & Ross James (9)
Sharmans Cross Junior School

The Rain Storm

Slowly it builds up darker and darker,
Coming together darker and darker,

Starts opening up quicker and quicker,
The heavens draw apart, quicker and quicker.

Then it leaps from the sky, like a paratrooper,
Homes in on its prey, like a peregrine falcon.

Hits the ground, with an almighty splash,
Makes everything wet, and everyone grumpy.

Slides down the hill, like a penguin on ice.
Into the drains, and mixes with the dirt.

Then stretches its legs, like a jumping frog.
Leaps towards the stars, and joins the real monsters.

Now comes the storm, lightning creating fires.
Punching things with its electrical arms,
Killing things and scaring people.

Crash comes the lightning from its evil arms,
Boom comes the thunder from its awful mouth,
Splash comes the rain from its tiny wet head,
And *aargh* go the children with their scared little minds.

As it dies down, people go outside.
They see all the water, and watch it as it dries.

Eventually, the sun beams down its beautiful hair.
And when the clouds look down,
They remember the fun they had last time.

Edward Thompson (11)
Sharmans Cross Junior School

Thunder Shock

The lightning tore through the sky
Roaring like a lion and setting fire to the trees
The thunder grumbled and growled
The wind grabbed the leaves off the branches.

Children playing, sprint inside
The lightning strikes everything it sees
The fire brigade too scared to come out
As the lightning spread to the town centre.

Without any warning it struck again
Which meant the ultimate in pain
The thunder roared louder and louder like an angry bear
Then faded away with a silent stare.

Phil Harrison (10)
Sharmans Cross Junior School

Waterfall Acrostic

W ater dropping from the waterfall
A nd becoming a river
T he water smashing rocks
E veryone seeing fish
R apid water smashing rocks
F ish in danger of rapids
A nd the river beginning to calm
L itres of water rushing to the sea
L ots of water spreading to the sea.

Conor O'Neill & Habeel Hussain (9)
Sharmans Cross Junior School

The Journey Of A River

Ice trickling off icicles into the water.
Running down the mountain into a gentle flowing stream
Until it meets the waterfall.
Gushing and thundering down into a gentle,
Peaceful bubbling stream.

In the distance I could see rapids zooming and howling.
I'm coming up to the rapids
Crashing and splashing down them.

Far ahead there was twisting and turning,
Erosion coming in from the left.
Spinning and curling,
Gurgling and gargling coming up to the meadows
And beautiful views.

Sheep and cows grazing
And coming to drink from the flowing water.
Up until the estuary opening wide meeting with the sea
At last the end of our journey
The crashing and splashing of the waves coming to a close.

Ben Stewart & Matthew Austin (9)
Sharmans Cross Junior School

River

R aging rivers rushing down the stream.
I cy drops crawl down the mountain to meet the raging river
V icious rivers terrify the people on boats.
E vil rivers gather rapid speed.
R ivers, rivers, rivers, icy cold.

Adam Griffiths & Richard Green (9)
Sharmans Cross Junior School

Pollution

From the top of the mountain
Where the river starts
There were beautiful views
I could see everything
The water flowed down the mountain
Into a beautiful stream
The river kept on going and flowing on
Then we saw people having a picnic
Left their junk behind
Then we saw oil
The water thickened up
Bottles in the water
Cigars on the bank
We came to a city
Pollution was high
The people were going crazy
Choked us up
At last we were out of that smelly city
Out we came into a beautiful estuary
Then we came out into the sea.

Jack Glendall (9)
Sharmans Cross Junior School

Soft, Calm River

R iver as calm as anything
 I n a world of its own
V iolent but calm
E ffort to be bad, but still calm
R eflection in the water
S ky reflecting down into the water.

Joe Reading & Sam Finnegan (9)
Sharmans Cross Junior School

Save Our Rivers!

I am a river,
I used to be shiny, beautiful and briny,
Now I'm ugly as a prune,
If you don't sort me out soon . . .
You won't have any water left, so there!

I'm a stream,
Ugly and green,
I used to be pretty,
But now I'm all bitty,
So . . .
Help me please!

We are the creatures that inhabit the river,
We used to be warm but now we shiver,
So . . .
If you don't do something we'll come and live in your bed!

Sam Russell & Sarah Low (10)
Sharmans Cross Junior School

Shower

S plash goes the water,
H ot water pouring down,
O n goes the tap, water's back,
W ater's pouring on me,
E nergy's back with a click and a clack,
R eady at last, down comes the rain I need a shower again.

Katie Smith & Sonam Kotecha (9)
Sharmans Cross Junior School

The River

The river slips over glistening stones
Scurrying round branches and rocks
Ice drips down onto the smooth surface
Causing small ripples
The slow dripping of water can be heard among the
Whistling wind.
The stream flows swiftly by and
Darts down the mountainside creating
A large pool of water among the woods and wildlife.
The river drifts through the forest and
Slowly but gradually travels through the countryside
The river is nearing the end of its journey down
The mountains, past the countryside and down to the sea.
And as it closes in upon the end I can sense the
Salty air as the river whooshes past me and into the sea.

Rebecca Chard (10)
Sharmans Cross Junior School

Untitled

Water trickling over the stones.
Weeds blowing in the wind.
Fish swimming here and there.
Fish jumping in the air.
Sunshine reflecting off the water.
People fishing on the bank.
Dogs swimming in the shallows.

Christian Lindsey & Callum James (9)
Sharmans Cross Junior School

Snow

It creeps at night getting faster,
Sprinting towards the town.
Not stopping, racing against time,
It's over us now silently it starts drifting down.
He throws the flakes down.

It starts falling heavily now.
He's leaping onto cars and trees.
Pouncing on anything in its way.
He glides around town nearly flying.

He starts coming down faster than before.
Slowly the ground piles up.
He's silent but sprinting fast, goes away.
We wake up and come out excited building snowmen,
Throwing snowballs while he runs away.

Jack Maddalena (10)
Sharmans Cross Junior School

The Sea

Crashing waves, leaping dolphins
Swishing tails of the sharks
The foamy sea is whooshing fast
The tide is coming in
Golden sand is turning brown
The flowing sea calming down
Active dolphins go to sleep
Scary sharks go to sleep
The sea goes to sleep.

Zoë Blackburn (9)
Sharmans Cross Junior School

Tornado

Rapidly turning on its way to the town,
Twisting and turning and swirling around.
People and pets scream and shout,
Watching as it throws the houses about.

The tornado dives and turns and leaps
Just like a child, it never wants to sleep.
Stamping on people, like it's a game,
And it makes people homeless, again and again.

The town no longer a town,
Just rubble for us to see,
No complete buildings, no complete families.

As the tornado hurtles on,
No clean water, or edible crops,
Everyone asking the same question,
Will it stop?

Hannah Hughes (10)
Sharmans Cross Junior School

Stormy Waves

Waves crashing on the beach
Knocking everything in its way
Splishing, splashing everywhere
Spraying water at people
Breaking before it reaches the shore
Dribbling foam in the sea
Gurgling noise it makes
Too rough for people to swim in
The waves higher than the sand dunes
Nearly going over the top
Calming down
As the waves get smaller
Until there are hardly any waves at all.

Charlotte Taylor (9)
Sharmans Cross Junior School

Rivers

It's glimmering
Shimmering
Divine
Beautiful
It's absolutely perfect!
It's sky blue
Trickling
Tickling the rocks
It's absolutely perfect!

It's lush
Calm
Plentiful
Shining
It's absolutely perfect!
It's everything you could want!

It's polluted
Disgusting
Ugly
Bleak
It's absolutely horrible!
It's pongy
Still
Eroding the rocks, dull
It's absolutely horrible!

It's overgrown
Mossy
Not enough
Black
It's absolutely horrible!
It's nothing you could want!

Radu Thomas (9)
Sharmans Cross Junior School

Vortex

The vortex comes sliding silently across the landscape,
His icy grey face looms over the city,
Ready to strike.

The vortex floats noiselessly down the hillside,
Towards the city,
The crackling, slipping, sliding,
Spreading like a disease.

The vortex comes drifting mutely across the countryside,
Freezing all in its path,
Screaming people struggling to get away.

The vortex glides speechlessly down the streets,
Skidding along, searching for a victim,
When will it stop?

Dominic Savin (10)
Sharmans Cross Junior School

Rivers

When the light blue river was gushing by
The birds were tweeting in the sky
The tiny ducks were floating around
When I heard a gurgling sound
I saw a silver fish
And then I made a wish
To come and see this lovely view
That will soon come true.

Faye Curley & Mary Potter (9)
Sharmans Cross Junior School

Pollution

Pollution floating on the river.
The greasy oil makes me shiver
Rubbish fills up half of the water
I think we need a rubbish sorter
This whole place stinks of litter
I think we need a river sitter
Everything here stinks of pollution
I think we need to find a solution
I hate this river because there is lots of rubbish
It smells very stagnant and looks very sluggish.
Pollution, pollution, I hate pollution.

Melissa Bulsara (9)
Sharmans Cross Junior School

Pollution

Pollution, pollution that's so bad
Pollution, pollution we need a solution
If you're not going far don't use a car
Rubbish is mean
We need to make it clean.

Jonathan Lawson & Sam Upton (9)
Sharmans Cross Junior School

Wave Acrostic

W aves crashing against bulging rocks
A nd the violent waves washing people away
V iolent storms are coming in quickly
E nd of the storm at last, peace at last.

Robert Comer (9)
Sharmans Cross Junior School

An Angel's Rainbow

Fingers tapping, on my windowpane
Pitter-patter, pitter-patter, falling heavy rain.
Feet stamping, on my windowpane
Pitter-patter, pitter-patter, tapping again and again.

I step outside, and feel the rain trickling down my face.
Glints of light, shining from its eyes
Grey clouds above me.
I feel refreshed and calm.

The sky cries, tears streaming down its lonely face.
I can smell damp air.
As the rain stops, the rays from the sun come out.

Then an angel flew across the sky,
And made a rainbow with the colours of a phoenix's tail.

Megan-Rose O'Boyle (10)
Sharmans Cross Junior School

Rivers

R ivers are fast and slow.
 I like the waves swishing past the rocks.
V ery slow and fast waves and rivers can do both.
E vaporating water from the sun.
R ivers flowing and waves tapping against the rocks.

Craig Sweeney (9)
Sharmans Cross Junior School

Waterfall

Crash, splosh, the water bashes against the ridged rocks
The waterfall slides down, *splosh, splish*
The water speed is like a racing car
Splash, splish, splosh.

Hanifa Kamal (9)
Sharmans Cross Junior School

The Galaxy Storm

I am a gentle breeze
Second by second I feel
Stronger and stronger
Minute by minute
Hour by hour
An extreme force is
Building within me
Now I can't stand
It anymore, I
Must unleash my power
I rip roofs off houses
I leave a trail of destruction
Behind me
I am so strong, I am so mighty.

After the terror has passed I am reduced to a simple breeze.

Servern Chana (10)
Sharmans Cross Junior School

Polluted River Poem

Polluted rivers
Kill fish
With oil lurking across the river
Forming into a monster
Glass bottles trapping creatures
Plastic bags, suffering fish.

Lee Scholes (9)
Sharmans Cross Junior School

Tornado

As it comes through the island it roars
Through houses and rips through
Furniture, slaughters the trees and belts
The cars, crushing lorries and savaging the
Buses. The huge powerful centre uplifts
Roads so tarmac flies through
The air grinding through
People's bones but the
Immense destruction
Doesn't go on
Forever
Because
It will
Eventually
Stop!

Jack Buttery (10)
Sharmans Cross Junior School

Waves

The hot waves, sunrise flowing continually onto my feet
And onto the golden sand.
The sky blue waves at midday against the golden sand
Like walking on a beach of gold.
The soft pattern of the orange waves
At sunset the yellow of the beach and the water.
The pitch-black waves at midnight twilight
Everlasting ongoing.

Alexander Miller (9)
Sharmans Cross Junior School

The Destructive Tornado

Tornado,
Flattening, stomping on passers by,
Spinning and ripping, demolishing everything in its sight,
Cars flying everywhere,
Its claws destroying homes,
Setting everything on fire,
Tearing and slashing, video cameras filming this bit of terror.

It's dangerous breath whipping people's faces,
Smashing people's homes,
Making everyone's life a complete misery.

Rain pouring down, tackling the monster,
Rain clouds hovering over the monster,
Spilling onto the cowering animal,
Tornado leaves,
Monster goes,
Tornado.

David Kurowski (10)
Sharmans Cross Junior School

Clean River

Fish swimming
All day long
Beavers working all night
Rivers so clean
You can see the bottom
No pollution
In this river
Waters flow
Near the bank
Swans swim
Peacefully.

Alex Robertson (9)
Sharmans Cross Junior School

The Wild Lightning Bolt

Slowly, he lingers behind the clouds,
Waiting for a victim to pounce on,
His gleaming, yellow eyes waiting to strike,
He approaches his prey with a spring.

His legs manoeuvring his body from behind the clouds,
He sprints through the sky,
Crashing into trees,
Boom, crash, falling to the ground.

Flashes in the sky, birds wildly flapping their wings,
It pounces and springs from one car to another,
People screaming running into houses,
Then, it slowly calms down.

It leaps behind the clouds,
Re-visiting all the damage he's done,
He sits back and relaxes,
Slowly closing his eyes.

I see the cars and trees,
All crashed and dented,
I turn the fire on,
And eat my mum's cottage pie.

Robbie Hadley (10)
Sharmans Cross Junior School

River

The sky blue, grass green river
Flowing in the daylight
Meeting the moonlight
Splashing everywhere it goes.

Joe Henrick (9)
Sharmans Cross Junior School

The Terrorising Tornado

A giant monster,
Smashing all in its path.
Crashing down skyscrapers,
Ripping up cars.

Like a colossal rhino,
Charging around a jungle.
Of huge metal trees,
Foraging slowly for food.

As the storm returns to its sleep,
And the sun comes out.
The rhino sprints away,
To return to its home.

Ollie Weaver (10)
Sharmans Cross Junior School

Polluted River Poem

Dark muddy water
Rubbish covering the slime stones of the filthy river
Black moody water
Fierce rapids crashing against the muddy rocks
Water soaks into the murky mud
Turns the water dark and grubby green
It's dangerous!
No one dares to go near.

Natalie Kent & Emma Doran (9)
Sharmans Cross Junior School

The Waves

The great green wave sailed across the ocean deep
Whilst the magical sun set.

A gentle wave slowly crashed into the rocks,
Others turned turquoise
As the sun was slowly driven upwards into the purple sky.

The shimmering waves glinted at the moon and soared past,
Rolled into the shore, melting in the golden sand.

Joseph Bartholomew (9)
Sharmans Cross Junior School

Waterfall

Pitch-black at midnight,
Delicate pale blue waterfall forces water down
Light of the moon reflects calm falling water
It crashes,
Splashes at the bottom
Then it carries its long slow journey again.

Millie Watling & Chloe Godding (9)
Sharmans Cross Junior School

Aqua Rivers

Aqua blue ripples
Washing over the bronze rocks
Glowing in the sunlight
Flowing down the waterfall
Huge trees hanging over the gentle river
Like hands playing in the water.

Evie Pinner & Sophie Jordan (9)
Sharmans Cross Junior School

The Day The Sun Came

Here comes the hottest day of the year again
Everybody rushes to the beaches
The sun, roaring down at the visitors
Swimming across the land
The heat, prowling across the beach
Lolloping itself across everybody
The sun so bright its shiny big teeth are showing
Scratching its furry golden mane
Here goes the hottest day of the year
The visitors returning home.

Megan Hill (10)
Sharmans Cross Junior School

Hurricane Winds

Blowing till its cheeks go red
Destroying everything in its path
Leaves whirling because of its strength,
That buzzing noise coming from its mouth
Staying in our heads for evermore.

The hurricane pushed a wave of people
Charging, charging
People left lifeless, people left homeless,
Due to the fierce, raging hurricane winds.

Helena Garnett (10)
Sharmans Cross Junior School

Blizzard

The sun has set
I can come out of my den.
Winter has finally come,
Hurry up my fellow friends,
We have to spread our disease once again.

I growl and snarl shaking my great white fur.
Swiftly moving through the town,
I freeze roof to roof, window to window,
As I kill the city with great coldness.

Watch me go!
Lethal and murderous,
Freezing everything I touch.
I cackle with laughter,
As I go back to my den,
Hiding, watching to strike once again!

Gina Tucker (10)
Sharmans Cross Junior School

Polluted River Poem

The dark brown water flows past
Until it reaches the polluted water,
The dead fish float up to the top of the dirty water
With trees collapsed in ongoing mucky green water
Floating about all you can see grubby green site.

Rohan Riches (9)
Sharmans Cross Junior School

The Foggy Night

The panther's mean
Quiet and low
Hunting for his prey
Through the dark gloomy night.

He spreads his damp mist
Blinding people so they can't see a thing
He creeps through the air
Ready to pounce.

Pressing against the windowpanes
He will not stop until morning
Quickly he returns to his den
And waits until it's night
To strike back again.

Patrick Holliday (10)
Sharmans Cross Junior School

Le Onde

Unending wave,
Long-lasting gentle wave,
The sky-blue wave was permanent.
The indigo wave was non-stop.

Elliott Hale (9)
Sharmans Cross Junior School

Foggy Night

Fog!
A creepy spectre
It glides through the city,
A ghostly vision
As it moans and moans.

Headlights of a car
Just like panthers' eyes,
It makes the fog luminous,
It crawls before suddenly pouncing
Wrapping itself around buildings
Not letting go.

The fog snake,
It slithers in the alleys and gullies
Creeping into dark corners,
So scaly, with a venomous bite,
It blocks out any light.

The fog spider
Creepy and crawly
Its deadly bite blurs your vision,
Blinding you
Finally the sun comes out
The fog is gone!

Adam Mercer (10)
Sharmans Cross Junior School

Weather Acrostic Poem

F rost cold as ice
R acing but I keep on slipping
O n the track it is very icy
'S teady!' the crowd said
T rying to win. Yeah *I did it.*

Catherine Sisman (8)
Sharmans Cross Junior School

The Mighty Storm

I am Storm
Dark and powerful, no one can destroy me
My thunder pierces the Earth
Lightning zigzags the sky with my sharp talons
There is just one mighty flash in the sky
My heavy black clouds pour down rain
Shooting down like darts

I am Storm
With just one puff of my breath
I tear off roofs
Street lights shatter as I howl to the sky
I am mighty
Powerful
It is only I who can cause this havoc
I am the greatest
Until . . . one last tear of rain falls
My time is up
But I will be back next time!

Darcy Scarlett (10)
Sharmans Cross Junior School

Snakey Rain

Snakey rain strikes again
Gently hissing on the windowpane
But snakey rain isn't the gentle type
So he gets his teeth ready to bite!
Harder and harder snakey gets
Banks are bursting!
The happy atmosphere is surely dead
Plants are suffocated with water!
Alas the sun has shone
Snakey rain has lost it's fun
No one but no one can defeat her!

Ameenah Ali (10)
Sharmans Cross Junior School

Storm

I am a storm
Thrashing thunderbolts with anger
Bursting clouds with a blow of breath
Rain coming, hitting anything in its way
Like a dart piercing onto the ground
Endless pain

I am Storm
Sending shivers down spines
As I blow trees and homes away
As I stop upon streets tearing roads apart
When I sleep, I snore and lightning hits the Earth
The sun is back
I slowly creep back to my lair
The sun has won
Till next time!

Adam Scholes (10)
Sharmans Cross Junior School

Wind Skater

The wind, like a skater
Twisting, turning
A shock, a strong vigorous force
Hurtles past

It dances, leaping to and fro
Whistling happily
To its own pleasure
A made-up tune

Hitting the trees with all its power
Falling, falling
Lost power dying down
It's finished.

Olivia Ford (10)
Sharmans Cross Junior School

The Blizzard Snow Queen

I am a powerful blizzard,
Creating sharp snowflakes,
I am the snow queen, not a wizard.

I create fast and strong snowstorms,
Everyone trembles in my presence,
Snow soaring down like extremely sharp horns.

I have ice-blue skin,
A long cloak, which blankets the Earth,
You will soon find out that I always win.

I am invincible, regal and strong,
People perish who get in my way,
Ice is my weapon, the wind is my song.

Oh no, the sun has come out,
I give the people my last icy stare,
Now I must slide home on the ice as I pout,
Now I am safe and cold in my lair.

Eloïse Brown (10)
Sharmans Cross Junior School

Mirror Poem

A hand
Wrinkled and jagged
Firm and lanky
Like an old prune
It's an autumn leaf
Like an old prune
Firm and lanky
Wrinkled and jagged
A hand.

Olivia Howse (8)
Sharmans Cross Junior School

Tornado Dragon

Tornado dragon, comes down to Earth from his planet lair.
And causes havoc upon our world.
He's terrifying, murderous and has no boundaries,
He does as he pleases, decimates our population.

Tornado dragon, he spins and twirls
Ripping up houses as he goes,
He kills sabotages all that we have made.
He smashes, causes pain and has no boundaries,
All he does is release his anger upon our planet.

Tornado dragon, he is invincible,
He'll not stop until all is gone.
He is lethal, shocking - has no boundaries,
This violent monster seems to be unstoppable.

Tornado dragon, just when all help is lost,
The sun god saves us all
Knocking the monster back to his fiery lair,
Everyone cheers,
But the tornado dragon will strike again.

Ryan Wilson (10)
Sharmans Cross Junior School

Mirror Poem

A hand
Rough and peeling
Cut and bloody
Like a rock
It's a builder's friend
Like a rock
Cut and bloody
Rough and peeling
A hand.

Jack Stanley (8)
Sharmans Cross Junior School

Starry Night

(Inspired by the painting 'Starry Night' by Van Gogh)

Starry Night
An empty and quiet countryside
A farmer gazing at the beautiful stars
Stars flickering frostily in the autumn midnight sky
Starry Night

Starry Night
Cyprus trees reaching up to the gloomy sky
Wavy stars in the dull, rough sky
Mushy snows falling slowly down the hills
Starry Night

Starry Night
Wind swirling like a slow tornado
People's voices echoing from the high hills
Feeling cosy in my snug bed
Starry Night.

Keryn Boyle (8)
Sharmans Cross Junior School

Kennings

Bone cruncher
Fish eater
Night hunter
Ship wrecker
Deep diver
Man hater
Human beater

Answer: One big shark.

Lucy Barnes (8)
Sharmans Cross Junior School

Starry Night

(Inspired by the painting 'Starry Night' by Van Gogh)

Starry Night,
A lost lonely village in the beautiful hills,
Farmers sleeping after working endlessly every day,
Autumn night, icy cold,
Starry Night.

Starry Night,
Cheerless and gloomy, blue and grey,
Curved and pointed silhouettes of wolves and foxes
Spiky, painted, rough cypress trees
Starry Night.

Starry Night
Dull and windy autumn night
Owls and wolves howling and hooting
Calm and relaxed as the sun goes down
Starry Night.

Zoë Carter (9)
Sharmans Cross Junior School

My Weather Poem

B ringing up snow as it turns,
L ike your warm heart, burns,
 I n elephantine, titanic caves.
Z apping strong wind waves,
Z ooming round and round,
A lump of snow in a mound.
R aging right past me,
D arting through freezing towns and terrible seas.

Miriam Farrant (8)
Sharmans Cross Junior School

Starry Night

(Inspired by the painting 'Starry Night' by Van Gogh)

Starry Night
Dreamy remote magical village
Villagers sleeping peacefully in their comfortable
Softly-lit houses
Starry Night.

Starry Night
Pitch-black midnight sky
Sharp pointy cypress trees
Bumpy and rough houses
Starry Night

Starry Night
Freezing storm and snow on the mountains
Deafening noise of lightning
Alone and scared
Starry Night.

Matthew Else (8)
Sharmans Cross Junior School

Kennings

High hopper
Ear flopper
Carrot eater
Night sleeper
Deep digger
Attention catcher
Tunnel maker
Eagle hater.

Answer: A rabbit.

Sian Last (8)
Sharmans Cross Junior School

Starry Night

(Inspired by the painting 'Starry Night' by Van Gogh)

Starry Night
I'm lost in a wide open spaced field
I'm an abandoned child
The clock strikes twelve as I tread through the slush
Starry Night

Starry Night
I notice a golden opal moon at the corner of my eye
Smudged stars in the sky
I can feel rough rolling hills
Starry Night

Starry Night
I feel cold as a gust of wind brushes through my hair
I can hear owls hooting an unloving sound
The snow drifts down
Starry Night.

Abigail Bates (8)
Sharmans Cross Junior School

Kennings

Tree swinger
Vine clinger
Rainforest hider
Fruit lover
Hunter hater
Friendly cuddler
Back scratcher
Tree climber
Banana eater

Answer: A big crazy monkey.

Hannah Guest (9)
Sharmans Cross Junior School

Starry Night

(Inspired by the painting 'Starry Night' by Van Gogh)

Starry Night
A dreamy village in the lost countryside
Tired farmers coming down from the farms
To give their milk away
People sleeping tightly
Starry Night

Starry Night
The bright white stars gleaming in the darkness
The curly wind, bashing against glass windows.
The lumpy mountains go on forever,
Starry Night

Starry Night
The gloomy sky lets out a bit of light
People shouting loudly keeps you awake.
Calm people all relaxed in their comfy beds.
Starry Night.

Christopher Lloyd (8)
Sharmans Cross Junior School

Weather Acrostic Poem

F rost sparkling laid on the grass so cold as a block of ice.
R ippling through the streets.
O n tree branches it glitters way up high.
S nowflakes come twinkling down so slowly.
T aking their time to fall to the ground.
Y ou and me feel nippy, soon we will be frozen.

Amy Canning (8)
Sharmans Cross Junior School

Starry Night

(Inspired by the painting 'Starry Night' by Van Gogh)

Starry Night
A village in France
I am spying watching for the mayor
It's autumn - dark and early
Clouds drifting away
Starry Night

Starry Night
Starry Night I can hear screaming
Footsteps behind me
I'm weak, cold and nervous
Starry Night

Starry Night
Starry Night, the swirly golden moon
Indigo sky, circles, bright, curved, twinkling stars
Swirly sky drifting north.
Starry Night.

Naomi Bury (8)
Sharmans Cross Junior School

Mirror Poem

The hand.
Wrinkled and uneven.
Shrivelled and lined.
Like a bristly piece of bark.
It's an eagle's claw scratching.
Like a bristly piece of bark.
Shrivelled and lined.
Wrinkled and uneven.
The hand.

Kathryn Parker (8)
Sharmans Cross Junior School

Mirror Poem

A hand

Wrinkled and tight
Veined and bony
Dry and cracked
Strong and gripped
Like ancient paper
It is a scorching desert
Like ancient paper
Strong and gripped
Dry and cracked
Veined and bony
Wrinkled and tight

A hand.

Madelyn Curnyn (9)
Sharmans Cross Junior School

A Hand

A hand
Freckled and pale
Short and flexible
Smooth and cold
Like a killing machine
It's a speckled cobra
Like a killing machine
Smooth and cold
Short and flexible
Freckled and pale
A hand.

Joseph Stevenson (8)
Sharmans Cross Junior School

Trapper Poem

T iredly I'm woken at 4am
R ushing to the mine at 5am
A bucket awaits as I go down
P anic, panic as the light disappears
P ersevering as the day goes on
E xhausted, I feel so empty
R ough and glad as the shattering day ends.

Tomorrow brings nightmare visions.

Felicity Zakers (10)
Sharmans Cross Junior School

Spooky - Haiku

Faint shadows glowing
Numb silhouettes of dull trees
Grey wolves chasing me.

Lucy Rutter (8)
Sharmans Cross Junior School

A Hurrier

H orribly woken at 4am
U nder the dark sky I run
R acing to get to the mine
R eally gloomy, as I enter the pit shaft
 I feel dizzy and weak
E ager to finish on time
R esting for another day.

Going down the next day, gives me horrible nightmares.

Jack Whitehouse (11)
Sharmans Cross Junior School

Starry Night

(Inspired by the painting 'Starry Night' by Van Gogh)

Starry Night
Looking from the trees in the blistery wind
The shepherd's standing on the hills.
Autumn dark and the misty white stars are twirling
Starry Night

Starry Night
A lemon moon glinting all around twirling,
A sinuous tree dancing and twisting,
A sharp point from the distance - as sharp as a needle.
Starry Night

Starry Night
Thunder clashing down
Wolves howling and rivers floating,
I feel lost in the cold
Starry Night.

Bethany O'Malley (8)
Sharmans Cross Junior School

Mirror Poem

A hand
Veined and bruised
Scratched and leathery
Like a sparkling fire
It is a stronghold
Like a sparkling fire
Scratched and leathery
Veined and bruised
A hand.

Ryan Pearson (8)
Sharmans Cross Junior School

Trapper's Terror

I swing down from the pit shaft,
It gets darker, darker, darker,
Smellier, smellier, smellier,
Colder, colder, colder it gets.

At the bottom you turn petrified,
Knowing you'll ache,
Sit wait, sit wait, sit wait,
Children whizz past with a big almighty wagon,
That's when I open the massive doors.

Work, I work 12 hours a day,
It seems everlasting.

I wait for the scary man to come,
He comes,
I get wound up like a twister,
I see the light,
It blinds me,
I wish I didn't have to go down again,
I feel exhausted,

I go down again . . .

Matt Povey (10)
Sharmans Cross Junior School

Mirror Poem

A hand
Veined and warm
Gentle and numb
Like a wrinkled hand of God
It's a stronghold for safety
Like a wrinkled hand of God
Gentle and numb
Veined and warm
A hand.

Fraser Waddell (8)
Sharmans Cross Junior School

Trapper's Tale

In the early morning's silence,
Coming to the pit shaft,
It's steep, so very steep,
The light getting further, further away,
Until, like transferring into another world,
You're submerged into the darkness.

Long corridors,
Getting narrower, narrower,
Ceilings getting lower,

Frightened
Sitting next to the huge door,
Nervously awaiting,
The thundering shudder of the almighty wagons.

Scent of the immense amount of coal,
Sight of the young children pulling the wagons,
Even younger ones pushing.

Relief of going back up,
Then the worry of going back down tomorrow.

Ellie Davie (11)
Sharmans Cross Junior School

Mirror Poem

A hand
Secure and hairy
Tight and warm
Like a cosy teddy bear
It's a holiday memory
Like a cosy teddy
Tight and warm
Secure and hairy
A hand.

Harry Floyd (8)
Sharmans Cross Junior School

The Trapper And The Wagon

The door is huge, twice my size
I'm nervous, confused, disrespected
I stay, wait, listen, think
What can I do? What can I say?
Nothing, nothing, nothing
Rattle
What?
Rumble
Door
Now
Done
'Who are you?'
My words lost in a cloud of dust
Water dripping on my head
Vibrations, vibrations, vibrations
Gone
Out of time
Another day over.

Tom Johnston (10)
Sharmans Cross Junior School

Mirror Poem

A hand
Skinny and veined
Cold and comforting
Like a freezer, but a little warm inside
It's a hot chocolate on a wintry day
Like a freezer, but a little warm inside
Cold and comforting
Skinny and veined
A hand.

Remy Prince (8)
Sharmans Cross Junior School

A Hurrier

Clang, clunk, clang,
The hewer hauls the coal into the corf,
Rumble, rattle, rattle, rumble,
I strain as I drag the corf,
The sharp pieces claw into my feet, slice them through.

I strain my eyes trying to see, it's impossible,
The corridor gets smaller, smaller,
Lower, lower, the air gets tighter.

A door swings open and I collapse,
Thwack, thwack, master whipping me.

I am exhausted, strained, I ache severely
Arms and legs bruised, sliced,
I flop to the floor, grazing my knees,
My fingertips are sore.

Hauling my body forward,
Hanging my head,
The light stings my eyes, tingling.

A great shot goes down my spine,
Tingle, tingle, tingle,
So sore, master dragged me through corridors.

Squeak, squeak,
The bucket winds me up,
The faded light becomes bigger,
The stale, musty smell blows away,
My eyes light up, my body is free.

The fresh wind blows into my face,
My eyes open wide,
They seem to shiver themselves,
Just about ready for another day,
In the mass of black.

Eleanor Webb (10)
Sharmans Cross Junior School

A Trapper's Day

I can hear trickling water
I can see nothing
I can feel the ground shivering
I can smell the stench of coal
I can hear a rattling.

I know a wagon's coming
I know I must open the door
I know he'll beat me if I don't
I know I don't want to but
I know I must

I am bored
I am tired
I am hurt
I am bitter cold
I am famished

I am not allowed a light
I am not allowed to sleep
I am not allowed to sing
I am not allowed lunch
I am not allowed to move from where I am

I'm sure if you did
I'm sure you wouldn't like it
I'm sure you'd get bored
I'm sure you'll get hurt
As a trapper.

William Chadwick (10)
Sharmans Cross Junior School

Down The Mines

I throw myself into the old rusty bucket,
I swing out,
The bucket rocks from side to side
Getting lowered down,
Knowing it's the last daylight I will see for 12 hours.
I reach the ground,
I feel worried,
Knowing when I come out I will be completely ineffective
As I walk down the narrow corridor,
The sound of coughing gets louder,
I walk through the dreaded doorway,
A man with a low accent says,
'Pick up an axe son,'
Walk further into the dull door,
I chop away at the coal,
Wouldn't dare talk,
Hooked to the dusty wagon,
Taste of dust in my mouth makes me feel sick,
Children coughing throughout the mine,
The chain around my waist yanking at my body,
I feel useless,
The smell of coal passes through your body
I hear the siren going through the mine,
Telling me my shift is over.

Jack Askey (10)
Sharmans Cross Junior School

Spooky - Haikus

Wolves howling, bats fly
I'm in a haunted mansion
Breathless I can't hide

I'm being followed
Faint footsteps I'm feeling weak
Shouting voices lost.

Sadie Fox (8)
Sharmans Cross Junior School

A Victorian Hewer

I wake up at 4 o'clock
I go down at 5 o'clock
It's a long queue
I climb into the massive bucket
As it sways side to side
I look up, the lights getting *smaller, smaller, smaller*
Knowing it will be another 12 hours
Until I'll see daylight again.

I walk to the end of the mine
The smell races against my face
I get to the end
I hack at the coal face
I place it into the wagon
I feel cold air rush into
The tears of my clothes.

I hear the loud sound of the siren
I walk to the bucket
I get wound up
I look down as the light blinds me
I wish not to go down there again
But I do . . .

Sean Keegan (10)
Sharmans Cross Junior School

Mirror Poem

A hand
Tiny and slippery
Sticky and tight
Like smooth silk
It is a mischievous child
Tiny and slippery
Sticky and tight
A hand.

Toby Lawrence (8)
Sharmans Cross Junior School

A Trapper's Life

5am
Everybody huddling together in the basket,
Down, down we go into the dreaded darkness.

7am
Down in the dark sitting next to my door,
I hear the corves being pushed and pulled,
I hear a corf coming my way,
Now it's my chance to play my part.

1pm
I'm shattered, I'm cold, longing to get home,
But I know there's only eight hours left of my hated work.

5pm
I'm sound asleep on the floor,
Now I hear the fearful footsteps of the overlooker,
Now I'm in trouble!

9pm
I'm so relieved, happy, joyful,
That it's time to go to bed,
I'm so glad my work is done!

12pm
I'm caught in a dream,
I can't wake up . . .
Asleep.

Hannah Burrows (10)
Sharmans Cross Junior School

Night Fright

(Inspired by 'I Met At Eve' by Walter de la Mare)

I met Night
He's not so bright
He gave me a scare
I had a nightmare

He has star eyes
As small as mini pies
The mouth's the moon
He looks like a baboon

He gives my window smash
In my eyes there's a flash
The Night's moving so fast
I haven't seen this in the past

In my nightmare he is hairy
Mostly he is scary
He wants to take me away
Poo! He smells like hay!

I met Night
He's not so bright
He gave me a scare
I had a nightmare.

Usman Ali (10)
Springfield Primary School

On The Way To School

In the morning as I was on my way to school
The world started to behave badly.
The cars began to cough and weep
As the bus went past if fell down
The lorry decided to moan and groan.
The sun was cooking the land.
The wind gets angry.

Hamza Iqball (11)
Springfield Primary School

Night After Dusk

(Inspired by 'I Met At Eve' by Walter de la Mare)

I met at dusk the godmother of night,
Her body filled with mystery and fascination
She crept closer with her slender arms and legs
Who has whispered the unspoken secret of the night?
No one escapes the phantom godmother of night.

Her sparkling eyes glanced from beneath her veil,
Flickering like transparent flames,
A beauty with rosebud cheeks
And her breath inhaling cold air,
Her lips looked like succulent strawberries
With a touch of glamour

Later when night goes the world wakes up with love
Leave our lovely lonely sky above the ground
Watching us with love and romance,
There on the clouds a jubilant godmother
Sleeping with comforting peace.

There we go again, I met the godmother of night,
Her body filled with mystery and fascination
She crept closer with her slender arms and legs
Who has whispered the unspoken secret of the night?
No one escaped the phantom godmother of night.

Arisha Masood (10)
Springfield Primary School

The Wind

When the wind is howling between the buildings
It is a dog looking for his lost puppy.

When the wind is pushing people
It is a dog breaking branches off a tree angrily.

When you hear a slurping noise
It is a dog drinking water.

Salma Nazir (10)
Springfield Primary School

Princess Of Night

(Inspired by 'I Met At Eve' by Walter de la Mare)

I met at dusk the princess of night,
Her beautiful, pretty face filled with mystery and fashion,
Her rosebud mouth opening and closing
She came closer and embraced me tight
And she whispered the unknown secret of the night.

Her sultry eyes glared at me,
Sparkling like transparent flames,
She felt like running and playing some games.

Her clothes long upon her feet,
I suggest she have a seat,
She'd rather say yes, maybe no.

Later when night goes the world wakes up with love,
Leave the lonely night and dance with romance in the light,
Princess resting with peace.

I met at dusk the princess of night,
Her beautiful, pretty face filled with mystery and fashion,
Her rosebud mouth opening and closing,
She came closer and embraced me tight
And she whispered the unknown secret of the night.

Nadra Shaheen (11)
Springfield Primary School

The Wind

When the wind is howling between the buildings
It is a dog, desperately looking for its lost puppies.
When the wind is whispering through the trees
It is an owl loudly howling in the night.
When the wind is pushing people
It is a loud thumping elephant.
When the wind is blowing at sea
It is a whale nudging the rocks.

Keertan Kaur Loha (10)
Springfield Primary School

Night

(Inspired by 'I Met At Eve' by Walter de la Mare)

I met at dusk the wizard of evil,
He was filled with mystery and wonder,
The wizard crept upon me and cast a spell to make me bright,
Then he whispered the secret of the night,
No one knew except for me,
No one escapes the wizard of evil

Due to an instant click of his finger,
He went through a secret passageway,
Which was covered with bushes,
That led to his hideous throne

Then the wizard came with his staff,
Then he brought all his raff,
Next he brought his crystal ball,
Which knows all

I met at dusk the wizard of evil,
He was filled with mystery and wonder,
The wizard crept upon me and cast a spell to make me bright,
Then he whispered the secret of the night,
No one knew except for me,
No one escaped the wizard of evil.

Adil Abbas (10)
Springfield Primary School

The Sun

Whenever the guests look at me I burn their eyes.
Whenever I go down the moon comes out and hurts me.
Whenever I go behind the buildings all the guests say goodbye
Whenever I am hungry I can't go down so I just eat the clouds
Whenever I vomit my vomit becomes a nice bright yellow
I am as big as the Earth and I don't have any skin - just
                                                    burning empty bones.
The last thing I do is give sunlight to the flowers.

Abbas Raza (11)
Springfield Primary School

The Busy Sun

The sun, the sun is the only one
Shines so bright it's having fun
It shines so bright it's like a glowing light.
It makes people hot so they decide to play
But then they get so tired they go back inside and stay.

The sun wakes up in the morning and falls asleep in the night.
The sun is in the sky
I wish I could sit on it to get there and fly,
But I know I'll burn to death without taking a breath.

The birds run past the sun and the sea walks under the sun
And when it's hot there's a lot of traffic
So there ends up being an angry mob of people.

The sun is bad but also good
It's supposed to be both, I'm sure it should
I like the sun I think everyone does.
Some people don't just because!

The sun, the sun is the only one shines so bright it's having fun.
It shines so bright it's like a glowing light.
It makes people hot so they decide to play
But then they get so tired they go back inside and stay.

Hasan Asmat (10)
Springfield Primary School

The Tree

When the winds blow my branches dance
When the sky cries it may wet me
I stand tall with my feet deep into the ground
My feet need water to pull me up
When the wind gets angry below me I lose my hair
When the wind pushes me
The cheeky monkey is finding his bananas
When the wind is whispering through me
The elephants fighting with their enemies.

Danyial Zafar (10)
Springfield Primary School

The Child Of The Night

(Inspired by 'I Met At Eve' by Walter de la Mare)

I met the child of the night,
His was a round and sparkling face.
He tiptoed up the steep rocky mountain,
Into the dark and lonely cave.
Where no soul dared to take a pace,
That's the child of the night.

His garb was gold,
About his eyes - they were almond-shaped and light blue.
He looked old but that was what he was told,
He loved to be seen.

His fragile skin was so smooth,
But people told him he should groove.
He's scared he might slip and fall into a thousand pieces
Like a porcelain figure.

He lives in a field,
Which used to have a great big shield.
He used to sleep in a bed,
But now he lives with his friend Ned.

I met the child of the night,
His was a round and sparkling face.
He tiptoed up the steep rocky mountain,
Into the dark and lonely cave.
Where no soul dared to take a pace,
That's the child of the night.

Hasib Elahi (10)
Springfield Primary School

Night Beauty

(Inspired by 'I Met At Eve' by Walter de la Mare)

I met at dusk the owl of the night,
Her face filled with joy and bright,
She came cautiously
Embraced me with her clear wings,
She held me tight
Uncovering the secret of the night.

She has clear skin like Snow White
She has red lips like my heart,
Almond full of generous water,
A mouth full of ice.

She doesn't move side by side
All she does is hide,
Then twilight falls,
Falls like a blanket,
Floats like a swan.

She lives in a house
Above the love
She will never leave the house,
It is the house of heaven.

I met at dusk the owl of the night,
Her face filled with joy and bright,
She came cautiously,
Embraced me with her clear wings,
She held me tight,
Uncovering the secret of the night.

Ikraam Samow (10)
Springfield Primary School

The Amazing Dark Night

(Inspired by 'I Met At Eve' by Walter de la Mare)

I met at dusk the child of night,
His face as soft as a teddy bear,
He moves around the forest here,
So lonely now he is,
The shiny moon he'd never miss.

His crystal eyes underneath his cap
He can't escape from the forest,
He needs a map.

His tiny feet no trainers wore,
His eyes glittered in their own flame.

His house in the hilly way,
Found out no one knew the name, of this little boy.

I met at dusk the child of night,
His face as soft as a teddy bear,
He moves around the forest here,
So lonely now he is,
The shiny moon he'll never miss.

Hibo Rashid (10)
Springfield Primary School

The Wind

When the wind is howling between the trees
It is a dog, desperately searching for its puppies.

When the wind is blowing the gate
It is a large elephant looking for food.

When the wind is blowing the sea
It is a jumping dolphin.

When the curtains are blowing it is the wind.
When the wind is blowing the paper, it is a flying seagull.

Faisal Nawaz (10)
Springfield Primary School

The Sun Is A Bun

The sun is bright,
The moon is light.
The stars shine at night,
But they are in our sight.

The sun comes up,
The sun comes down.
The sun is a round cup,
That makes no sound.

The sun is fun,
And the stars are boring.
The sun is a circle bun,
And the stars are snoring.

The sun is gold,
But seems very bold!
The moon is on hold,
But the stars are cold.

The sun is bright,
The moon is light.
The stars shine at night,
But they are in our sight.

Mohammed Ameer (10)
Springfield Primary School

The Wind

When the wind is howling between the buildings
It is a fox searching for food.

When the wind is pushing people
It is an elephant looking for water.

When the wind is blowing at sea
It is a lion roaring at the sea.

When the wind is breaking branches.
It is a chimp finding bananas.

Hafeez Aslam (10)
Springfield Primary School

Bite Night

(Inspired by 'I Met At Eve' by Walter de la Mare)

I met at dusk the king of night,
His face filled me with evil and wonder,
He crept closer with fear taking over my dreams,
He grabbed me tight saying the secret of the night.
I gave up without a fight, knowing I shouldn't take his might.
No one escapes the daring gracious king of night.

Undoubtedly his gleaming red, creepy, bulging eyes
Watched me beneath his gloomy mask with mystery
A dark blurry face with a strongly pealed smile
The staring face took my breath away with a mystical growl.

His looming skin sunk my heart with darkness
And his devouring name filled my lungs with a flame.

His house was in the mountain
Where the source of the river flowed.
A house of destruction with soggy walls
Whose orders would be obeyed whenever he called
For the moon sang and sang whenever he roared.

I met at dusk the king of night,
His face filled me with evil and wonder,
He crept closer taking over my dreams,
He grabbed me tight saying the secret of the night.
I gave up without a fight knowing I couldn't take his might.
No one escapes the daring gracious king of the night.

Owais Rehman (11)
Springfield Primary School

King Of Night

(Inspired by 'I Met At Eve' by Walter de la Mare)

I met the king of night,
His face a nice complexion,
He crept to me tiptoeing and embraced me,
There was no getaway from him,
He looked at me with his pale face,
He said no one escapes the king of night.

His wrinkly eyes glanced at me,
His face was veiled with a black scarf,
He came up to me like fire,
He is the one and only cruel man in the world.

He the king of night, was as breathtaking as running a mile,
He was as eerie as a ghoul in the night
It is almost as though you can see him invisible!
His skin is really smooth,
Why he did not want to groove?
He stood high and looked down,
For he was flying into the air.

I met the king of night,
His face a nice complexion,
He crept to me tiptoeing and embraced me,
There was no getaway from him,
He looked at me with his pale face,
No one dared to take a pace,
He said no one escapes the king of night.

Mohammed Hanif (10)
Springfield Primary School

The Evil Night

(Inspired by 'I Met At Eve' by Walter de la Mare)

I met at the deep, deep meadow the lady of the evil night
Her face was filled with spookiness and mystery,
She crept carefully and embraced me tightly,
She whispered hair-raising words deep in my ear
Escape the lady of night no one can!

Her eyes were sharp and ghastly shaped
Breathtaking was her evil face,
No one can escape these dreams,
No one has seen them except for me.

She rushed through the sparkling clouds.
Crept up to me and opened her big mouth,
I must fight the lady of the night
I must fight again.

Eat me she must not do
Fight the lady of the night
Again I must do it.
No one can escape her, no one, but I can.

I met at the deep, deep meadow the lady of the evil night
Her face was filled with spookiness and mystery,
She crept carefully and embraced me tightly
She whispered hair-raising words deep in my ear
Escape the lady of night no one can!

Anfal Ali (10)
Springfield Primary School

The Wind

When the wind is howling between the buildings
It is a wolf desperately searching for its prey
When the wind is angrily blowing
It is a lion searching, searching for its cubs.
When the wind is whispering through the trees
It is a cheeky monkey looking for its bananas.
When the wind is pushing people,
It is a loud elephant searching for its food.
When the wind is making a draught in the house
It is a nice sweet parrot tweeting, tweeting.
When the wind is carrying dandelion seeds along
It is a creeping, sneaking fox passing by.
When the wind is blowing flicking flowers
It is a deer running faster than lightning.
When the wind is blowing umbrellas inside out
It is a giraffe thinking the umbrella is food.
When the wind is blowing over the sea
It is a whale splashing making waves,
When the wind is blowing over a fountain
It is an elephant shooting water out of its trunk.
When the wind is blowing in the night
It is an owl sitting in a hole in the tree.

Reece Landa (10)
Springfield Primary School

The Man Of The Night

(Inspired by 'I Met At Eve' by Walter de la Mare)

I met at dawn the mysterious man of the night,
His face was as brave as a lion, fierce as a cat
He crept closer and coldly
He scared the lights out of me, his face was cold-blooded!

He grabbed me tight in his hand
My face, ears, mouth were watering.
I was asking for mercy but he didn't let me go
I couldn't slide through his hands
There was no way out or no way in
I was trapped with darkness all around me
The night moved steadily and calmly
It spread its wings all around
Spread the wonder of the land
Spread freedom around the world.
Then it settled in the sky where it rested calmly.

The night lives in the sky and it rests
No one can hurt it, no one can destroy it
It's there forever, you can't destroy it, I can't destroy it!
Who knows, who cares, it is the darkness of the world.

I met at dawn the mysterious man of the night
His face was brave as a lion, fierce as a cat
He crept closer and coldly.
He scared the lights out of me, his face was cold-blooded!

Wasim Hussain (10)
Springfield Primary School

The Wind

When the wind is howling between the buildings
It is a dog searching for its food.
When the wind is whispering through the trees.
It is a squirrel silently hopping around,
When the wind is pushing people
It is a lion searching for its cubs,
When the wind is blowing on the sea
It is a seagull looking for a fish to eat.
When the wind is pushing the trees
It is a cheeky monkey trying to eat his bananas
When the wind is making a cold draught
It is a polar bear creeping.
When the wind is breaking branches off a tree
It is a lion roaring,
When the wind is blowing
It is a giraffe hiding behind the trees.
When the wind is creeping
It is a lovely beautiful dolphin.
When the paper is blowing
It is a rat quietly creeping.

Sumera Athter (10)
Springfield Primary School

The Wind

When the wind is howling between the buildings
It is a dog playing with his puppy.
When the wind is whispering through the trees
It is a monkey searching for his bananas.
When the wind is pushing people
It is an angry lion roaring for his cubs.
When the wind is blowing at the sea
It is a stealthily moving wolf.
When the wind is making a cold draught
It is a creeping deer.

Adiba Khuram (10)
Springfield Primary School

The Night Place

(Inspired by 'I Met At Eve' by Walter de la Mare)

I met at dusk the queen of night
Her face filled with joy and happiness
She slowly crept upon me,
Embraced me with her soft, woolly coat.
She bound me tight with her slender arms.
She released her secret of the night.
No one knows except for me
No one escapes the phantom queen.

Pale eyes stared towards me,
Flickering snowballs rushing to me,
A delicate face with rosebud cheeks.
I don't know what I seek
She has a sensuous mouth
Like rain coming from a spout
No one escapes from the phantom queen.

She moves side by side, then she starts to hide
She creeps upon everything she sees.
Then she attacks like a swarm of bees
No one knows except for me,
No one escapes from the phantom queen.

She lives in a house above, full of love,
She has no food so she steals it
No one knows except for me
No one escapes from the phantom queen.

I met at dusk the queen of night
Her face filled with happiness and joy
She slowly crept upon me,
Embraced me with her soft, woolly coat.
She bound me tight with her slender arms
She released her secret of the night
No one knows except for me
No one escapes from the phantom queen!

Aliya Yousaf (10)
Springfield Primary School

The Mysterious Creature Of The Night

(Inspired by 'I Met At Eve' by Walter de la Mare)

I met at dark deep meadows, the creature of the night
His face filled with dreams and laughter
Slithering closer and deeper like a snake on the grass
He scared me right speaking the secret words of the night
I had no grip within his powers
No one escapes the creature of the night.

His hypnotising eyes stared towards me
Flickering like fire.
A black beauty with a lop-sided mouth
Breathtaking was his presence.

Slithering like a shadow of the night
Waiting to catch his prey while he looks
At the moon as bright as a torch light.
He runs like a cheetah with his crazy new tactics.

He creeps on people like a man giving you a scare!
He lives in oak trees so beware!
Flying on rooftops he does, he does
Looking for his prey and on he goes.

I met at dark deep meadows the creature of the night
His face filled with dreams and laughter
Slithering closer and deeper like a snake on the grass
He scared me right speaking the secret words of the night
I had no grip within his powers
No one escapes the creature of the night.

Nisba Ali (10)
Springfield Primary School

The Wind

When the wind is breaking branches off a tree
It is a gorilla, desperately searching for its bananas
When the wind is carrying a dandelion seed along
It is a squirrel, desperately searching for its nuts,
When the wind is whispering through the trees
It is a bee, flying around searching for its honey,
When the wind is blowing umbrellas inside out
It is an elephant looking for its peanuts.
When the wind is flicking flames in a fire.
It is an owl blowing the flames to catch its food.
When the wind is blowing at sea
It is a shark sniffing for blood.

Abdul Azeem (10)
Springfield Primary School

The Tree

I stand tall with my enormous feet deep in the ground
Reaching out, searching for water to quench my thirst.

Every time I feel the cold, I begin to lose my hair.
I hear the leaves crunch when I walk past the deep ground.
I feel bold when the leaves crunch.

As I walk the cold comes up to my brain
And I'm so hungry I have a stomach ache.

The cold rumbles on my feet when I walk past the ground.
At last I find an apple tree it rumbles and tumbles its leaves.

Zeeshan Hussain (11)
Springfield Primary School

The Wind

When the wind is howling between the buildings
It is a dog looking for its puppies,
When the wind is whispering through the trees,
It is a rabbit gently making a hole,
When the wind is pushing people,
It is a lion creeping behind trees,
When the wind is blowing the sea,
It is a seagull angrily looking for fish,
When the wind is pushing the trees,
It is a cheeky monkey swinging on branches,
When the wind is making a cold draught,
It is a polar bear shivering in the house.
When the wind is blowing the ocean,
It is a white whale looking for food.
When the wind is pushing the gate,
It is an elephant stamping his feet,
When the wind is breaking branches off the tree,
It is a giraffe looking for its baby,
When the wind is creeping,
It is a lovely dolphin.
When the wind is blowing,
It is a rat, creeping around,
When the wind blows the cheese
It is a mouse desperately hungry.

Thabat Laamache (10)
Springfield Primary School

The Wind

When the wind is howling between the buildings
It is a wolf.

When the wind is whispering through the trees
It is a wolf looking for its cubs.

When the wind is hurrying along
It is a deer quietly running along

When the wind is roaring loud
It is a raging lion, raging about.

When the wind is making a cold draught
It is a bird flapping its wings.

When the wind is breaking trees
It is a devouring hyena.

When the wind is screeching loud
It is a wolf calling its mates.

Masud Alam (10)
Springfield Primary School

The Tree

As the wind blows me, the leaves on my branches
Crumble off and crunch on the floor.
When I look at the sun the leaves on my branches
Start to burn and my skin cracks off.
When it's winter I stand in the breeze with my feet bare,
Deep into the ground and I begin to lose my hair.
I then search for some water to quench my thirst.
When it gets dark I start to droop because I'm getting too old
And I need a nice nap for the morning to come.

Sana Rehman (10)
Springfield Primary School

Where Do All The Teachers Go?

Where do all the teachers go?
When it's six o'clock
Do they live in bungalows?
And do they wash their frocks?

Do they wear tops?
And do they watch TV?
Do they scratch their ears?
The same as you and me!

Do they live with people?
Have they got mums and dads?
And were they ever children?
And were they ever sad?

Did they never draw right?
Did they make mistakes?
Did they not revise for the tests?
And were they ever pests?

Did they ever lose their science books?
Where they ever bad?
Did they scribble on the wall?
Did they have old dirty heads?

I'll follow one home today
I'll find out what they do
I'll put it in a poem
So that they can read it to you.

Sanah Akram (10)
Whitehall Junior School

An Animal Alphabet

A is for ant running up a tree
B is for buffalo shouting, 'Save me!'
C is for cat who got chased by a dog
D is for deer who fell over the log
E is for eagle flying like mad
F is for frog who loves his dad
G is for giraffe getting teased by rabbit
H is for hare whose friend is a maggot
I is for iguana who loves to eat
J is for jaguar who loves to cheat
K is for koala dancing like mad
L is for leopard always sad
M is for mouse eating cheese
N is for newt easy to please
O is for octopus who's got a bad mouth
P is for panda who lives in the south
Q is for queen-bee bossing everyone about
R is for rabbit whose hobby is to shout
S is for snake eating mice
T is for turtle; oh he's so nice
U is for ugly-duckling who goes to school
V is for very distressed dog who lost his tool
W is for whale swimming far away
X is for Xanthus who never had to pay
Y is for yeti who lived in the sky
Z is for zebra who ate a pie.

Sarba Khalid (10)
Whitehall Junior School

Aliens Stole My Golden Ring!

Aliens stole my golden ring!
I really don't know why
Probably it was real gold,
And they wanted to buy.

Aliens stole my golden ring!
I've always wondered why
Now I'm really, really upset
I just want to cry.

It was really, really cool
And very, very bald
I don't know where they have taken it
It's probably been sold!

Aliens stole my golden ring!
My fiancée has gone mad,
My dad has become rough
My mamma is really sad.

Here's a message for the aliens
'Hey you ugly bugs!
Next time you come round!
Just leave my friggin' jugs!'

Hamzah Butt (10)
Whitehall Junior School

Old Mother Hubbard And Her Dog

(Inspired by the nursery rhyme 'Old Mother Hubbard')

'Old Mother Hubbard went to the cupboard,
To give the poor dog a bone;
When she was there the cupboard was bare,
The poor dog had none.'

She went to the bakers to buy him some cakes,
When she came back the dog was in the lake.

She went to the Fish 'r' Us shop to buy a fishing net
When she came back the dog had a pet.

She took a clean bowl to get the dog some cake
When she came back the dog was a fake.

She went to the chemist to buy a sleeping pill,
When she got back
The dog was on a hill with a boy called Phil.

She went to the pub to buy him some brew,
When she got back he was wearing the lady's shoe.

She went to the shoe shop to get a new pair of shoes
When she got back the dog had the flu.

She went to the blacksmith to buy him a ring,
When she got back the dog was eating a chicken wing.

She went to a market to buy a mat to dance on
When she got back the dog was in France.

The lady heard a bark it came from her dog,
The dog barked and barked which meant,
'You old hag the dog is in your bag.'

The lady did a curtsy the dog did a bow,
The lady said, 'I'm your servant.'
And the dog said, 'Bow wow.'

Roxanna Naqvi (10)
Whitehall Junior School

Aliens Stole My Bike

To understand the ways
Of alien beings is hard
And I've never worked it out
Why they landed in my backyard.

Why do you think the aliens came for my bike?
When they could steal others
The aliens stole my bike
And took it back to their mothers.

Why did they come on Sunday night?
When I was tucked nicely in bed
The aliens took my bike
I'm sure one of them touched my head.

Mr Lee from next door
Caught them in the act
He saw the aliens take my bike
He said it was a fact.

I thought they were quite picky
When I saw nothing else was taken
I think aliens ride bikes
Or I think they were forsaken.

In the end they returned my bike
All dented and damaged
I don't know how they did it
But I'm sure that they managed.

Tyler Price (10)
Whitehall Junior School

Aliens Stole My PlayStation 2

To understand the ways
Of alien beings is hard.
And I've never worked it out
Why they landed in my backyard.

I've never found out why
On the journey from the dark
These aliens stole my PS2
And I followed them to the park.

They came on a Saturday night
When the PS2 is on all day
Ready to play for my brother and me
I went for 5 seconds and they said, 'Go away.'

Miss Rumbole from next door
Was a witness at the crime
When aliens snatched my PS2
That PS2 was mine.

It seemed they were quite choosy
As nothing else was in their vision
Do aliens play PS2?
And they forgot the television.

Now I've got it back
I play it every day
I never leave it alone
And I never go away.

Lee Jones (10)
Whitehall Junior School

The Teacher's Day In Bed

Our teacher's having a day in bed -
She's sent her pets to school instead!

There's . . .

A cockatoo to read the register,
A viper fish to sharpen the pencils,
A budgie to teach singing,
A centipede to teach maths,
A squid to make the ink,
An armadillo to hoover the floor,
A mouse to make the computer work,
A monkey to look for trouble at the back,
A puma to keep order at the front,
An ape (can't you guess to help with reading of course!)
An owl with glasses to run the office,
A shark to give swimming lessons,
(Glad I'm off swimming today!)
An angelfish to help with crossing the road,
A godzilla for entertainment,
A diplodocus to teach history,
A goldfish for golden time,
A bookworm for storytime,
A cheetah to teach PE,
An orang-utan to teach science,
I bet that none of you ever knew,
Just how many things a teacher can do!

Sarah Arshad (10)
Whitehall Junior School

Mr Bean And Teddy Discussing About The Future

'Oh Teddy I like this pretty woman
Why doesn't anyone like me?
I'm handsome and good-looking
I think she hates me because I lost her door key.

Everyone thinks I'm stupid and rude
She's got a dress which is white
I think she is saving it till we get married
But I just want to spend my life with her at night.

Her skin is a lovely shade
She has long silky black hair
Her face is full of beauty
And all I will do, will be to take care.

They say I can't help myself
I just love her so much
She's a great woman
But she thinks I speak Dutch.

It's not my fault I'm handsome
At least I've got someone to marry
She's really pretty
Because her name is Carrie.'

Jagdeep Mahal (10)
Whitehall Junior School

Aliens Stole My Cricket Set

To understand the ways
Of alien beings is hard.
And I've never worked it out
Why they landed in my backyard.

And I've always thought why
They made a big pattern,
The aliens stole my cricket set
And took it back to Saturn.

They came on a Thursday night
When I left it outside,
It was wet and not dry
I left it in my backyard.

Mr Frog from next door
Was a witness at the scene,
When the aliens snatched my cricket set
I was hoping that it was clean.

It seems that it was hard
As nothing seems to bat,
Do aliens play cricket
Or did they forget?

Muddasar Zaman (10)
Whitehall Junior School

Mr Bean And Teddy Discussing Feelings!

'Oh Teddy, I can't say it, I like her,
How can anyone like me?
I'm so clumsy, stupid and rude
Oh she is just going to flee.

Her skin is a lovely shade
She has long black hair
I just pick my nose
And then I've got you to care.

I don't have any money
I just wear this baggy suit
I always behave like a little kid
And now look there is a hole in my boot.

I live in this stupid flat
And all I do is *sob! Sob! Sob!*
Don't care about anything else
Anyway I don't even have a job!'

'No need to cry my friend
Remember I'm here for support
All you need is to tell her how you feel
That's it really, all you need is a bit of thought!'

Talha Nadat (10)
Whitehall Junior School

Bart And Lisa Discuss Good Grooming

How can you be so clever?
With a brain so small
Although you act so stupid
But I can kick a ball.

Your eyes are so round
Your hair is really silky
Your lips are so thin
And you smell really milky.

I envy your food
You tell the truth
You look really pretty
When you're in a great mood.

I love the music that you play
It goes like *da da de di*
The notes run by me
When you go *ma ma me mi.*

No Bart you're the greatest
It's true I've got round eyes
And I tell the truth
But would you like some apple pie.

Aiysha Akbar (11)
Whitehall Junior School

The Teacher's Day In Bed

Our teacher's having a day in bed
She's sent her pets to school instead.

There's . . .

A dolphin to teach swimming
A lion to tidy up after the children
An iguana for producing ink
A cave woman for history
A sparrow for geography
A whale for mixing paint
A millipede for maths
A rattlesnake for music
A kangaroo for picking up rubbish
A worm for producing silk
A spider for pulling books along
A phoenix for singing
A peacock for art
A hyena for sharpening pencils
Oh and a dragon for cooking.

Sally-Anne Cowley (10)
Whitehall Junior School

Harvest Time Is Coming!

Harvest time is coming
There's lots of food to share
Everybody gets some
Just to make it fair.

If people buy from a store
It will help the poor even more.
Harvest time is coming
There's lots of food to share.

Manraj Dhaliwal (9)
Woodfield Junior School

Plenty

Plenty of fruit,
Food and vegetables,
Lots of food to share,
Lots of food that the farmers grow,
We are so greedy; we don't give a care,
For those that don't have enough,
Hunger is winning them over.
They are hungry, starving, dying,
And we just stand there wasting it,
Like throwing money down the drain.
They don't have enough food,
And we all have too much.
They die because they don't have enough,
All the food that we wasted could have been there,
They still could all have been alive.

Nisha Patel (9)
Woodfield Junior School

Plenty

We have plenty,
We have enough,
Some don't have any, not enough.
I wish we had a world with no hunger or starving people.
So everybody gets enough at the harvest.
We are bountiful,
We are copious,
I wish there was enough to share it all.

Billy Geeson (9)
Woodfield Junior School

Plenty

Most people have plenty
Stocking up for harvest
Not bothering to share
Too greedy to care
Plenty of fruit and vegetables and water
We are so greedy that all we do with
The food that we can't eat is put in it
The bin
Not bothered about other people
And farmers grow crops and things like that
People cry out to us and beg for food
And all we do is ignore them
They beg for money, they beg and beg,
But as long as we have got more
Than them we don't care
We have a bounty of everything
Cakes, cookies and things like that,
They are dying of hunger and are starving to death.
While we watch and stand with all that food we wanted
Some are lucky to be more fortunate and some are
Unlucky and have been less fortunate.
We are so greedy
And we don't care
We are so greedy.

Sabeeya Walker
Woodfield Junior School

Plenty

The years harvest, bountiful,
Full of lovely fruit and veg,
This years harvest was plentiful,
So the farmers can have a rest.
We have enough to store as well as eat,
We could sell some,
It's the best harvest yet.

Darius Walton (9)
Woodfield Junior School

Plenty

It's harvest time
Time to collect the crops
Cabbages and carrots,
Potatoes and corn.
We will have loads of bread and cakes.

Loads of food to eat
Yum! Yum!

This harvest we have more than enough
We will share the plentiful harvest
Loads of apples and pears to eat
We are lucky we have food on our plates
Loads of rhubarb to make crumble.

Loads of food to eat
Yum! Yum!

Let's share our plentiful harvest around!
This has been a good harvest!
It's a shame some food will go to waste.

Olivia Jennings
Woodfield Junior School

Plenty

We have lots
Some don't have much
We have a plentiful supply of food.
Some don't have anything,
Our greed is high.
Their greed is low.
We have good harvests,
They have bad harvests.
We've got fantastic crops
They've got bad crops.
We are so lucky.

Tobias Pugh (10)
Woodfield Junior School

Plenty

I have lots and lots of food, all on my harvest growing.
I have bread and wheat and a great big feast.
A pear and an apple, both in my fruit bowl
And also an orange too.
I have vegetables and chocolate
And they both live in a fridge.
I also have my favourite, raspberries in a bowl.
I have more than others and more than enough
And I get it all from the corner shop.
I have strawberries and strawberries,
Lots and lots of them.
We also have raspberries too.
There is nothing else you would like because I have got it all.
I bet I am quite greedy, with all this stuff.
Some people have none and some have not enough.
I have plenty.

Florence Morgan
Woodfield Junior School

Plenty

We have enough to last us days,
They have enough to last them an hour,
We put them in our cupboards
They carry them in their trembling hands
We have plenty
They have none
We are guilty
They are innocent.

Luke Hedges (9)
Woodfield Junior School

Plenty For Everyone

Britain is a very plentiful country
With lots and lots to eat,
We have a fantastic harvest each year,
Of vegetables, fruit and meat.

We are a very fortunate country,
With lots to go around
We're always sufficient with food from above
Or beneath the ground.

We've surplus to requirements and everyday needs
We always have a generous amount
But we all have our greed!

Zoë Johnson (9)
Woodfield Junior School

Plenty

Sometimes we have plenty to eat,
Most of the time we have more than enough.
The thing that is bad is that we throw it to waste,
Not thinking about others that need it most.
So we should think about others,
And try not to throw it to waste.

Nathanael Hutchinson
Woodfield Junior School

Plenty

Plenty to eat, but plenty left over.
No more left for the poor people.
People are buying too much, far too much.

If people shared their food, we would need less.
If we stay like we are now, the world will end shortly.

Daniel Ward (10)
Woodfield Junior School

The Harvesters

Some families cannot feed.
Those who are more fortunate,
Food was put to misuse.

Greedy people store food,
When they need food it's rotted away
They purchase a bounty of food
They have more than enough.

Food is taken by people's greed
They cannot accept the rest
The food grown turns into dust
It rots in their homes and that's a waste of time.

Joshua Carr (9)
Woodfield Junior School

Plenty

It is autumn and the farmers are gathering up their crops
Most of the time we have a plentiful harvest.
Unlike some people far away, who hardly ever have enough
Who starve when there is not enough.
We always eat more than our share.
We are greedy.
We never think that out there somewhere,
People are starving to death.

George Simpson (9)
Woodfield Junior School

Plenty

This year's harvest was plentiful,
We had more than the last,
We have enough to fill up our stores.
We might even have enough to sell some of it,
We could even have had,
The best year yet!

Let's buy some more plants,
Let's buy some more land,
A rubber tree would grow quite quickly
If we invest in our plants,
Then we could become really rich,
And we should buy some exotic food.

Stephen Matthews (9)
Woodfield Junior School

Plenty

Britain over indulges.
Everything we see we eat,
We all have more than enough.
We are very ravenous,
But always have more.
We have a generous supply of food, all year round.
We are very greedy.
We store our food ready to share with others,
We fill up our cupboards with everyday needs,
Food all fresh,
From the corner shop.
For every tea we always have excess from it all.

Lily Dixon (9)
Woodfield Junior School

Lots Of Food

I have lots of food in my fridge,
Like ice cream, chocolate, grapes.
I don't really need this stuff, but I like it.
I buy all this from the store down the road.
I have all this money to spend,
Thousands and thousands of pounds.
I have family, lots of family.
I am grateful, I get everything I want.
Because we are lucky, we never starve.
We can have a long life -
So
Live it!

Abigail Blower (9)
Woodfield Junior School

Plenty To Eat

We have lots of food,
Like fruit and vegetables.
We all have a great big feast, at night-time
At harvest lots of people have enough food and drinks.
All of us have a good time,
There are other people who do not.
I feel sorry for the ones without any food,
But we can go to supermarkets.
I have lots of money for food.
We are greedy.

Amy Hillyard (10)
Woodfield Junior School

Plenty For Everyone Here

I have to stock up for the harvest
Get everything ready, I need to get more, get loads.
We are more fortunate.
We have a lot to eat.
The food is chocolate, cake and jelly.
We don't need this food, but we like it.
We have perfect drinks like wine,
Water, apple juice and orange
This food and drink we get from the corner shop.
This food I need for the family.
We work so hard for the money to buy.
So why should we share it?
Life is good so live it!

Somerset Smith (9)
Woodfield Junior School

A Bountiful Harvest

In the harvest we've plenty to eat,
So we share our food with the people we see.
We give them plenty so they do not run out!
We have run out so we need some more!

We are very, very generous to share our food.
So we never run out.
We give to our friends and family if they do not run out.

Ranjeet Bhogal
Woodfield Junior School

Plenty

The crop of the harvest is ready to pick.
We are very fortunate to have some,
We have enough, more than enough.
Too much to eat.
Some of the food in our fridge and our cupboard
Are ice cream, grapes, bread, butter, milk, chocolate,
Orange juice and apple juice.
It is very, very tasty I suppose we are quite greedy
To have all this food, we get it from the corner shop down the road.
Why should we share, we work really hard?
To get food on the table for our family
We are lucky we don't starve
Live, life forever.

Elizabeth Rushbury (9)
Woodfield Junior School

Good Harvest

It will be a bountiful harvest
Lots to share.
Sufficient harvest for everyone.

There's excess but no greed
Abundance with food for all.
Plenty of rice, bread and wheat.

We don't refuse visitors at harvest time.
For those in need
We will give food and health,
Maybe some wealth at harvest time.

Gabriel Walton (9)
Woodfield Junior School

Too Much Harvest

Farmers plant the millions of seeds
And wait for half a year
But we have too much,
Because other countries don't have enough.
For we have plenty and a sufficient store of food.
And they don't have enough.
Most of our food goes to waste.

Luke Stavenuiter (9)
Woodfield Junior School

Plenty

The farmers in the field have grown plenty
It's all stacking up for people to have
There is more than enough for others
There is lots and lots of food
The people have greed and want more
At the end there will be lots left.

Jayna Patel
Woodfield Junior School

Plenty

Most of the time we have more than we need,
We don't think about others,
Those who need it more than us.
The bad thing is we throw it to waste,
And we don't think about others who need it most.

Rajan Halaith (9)
Woodfield Junior School

Plenty

When it is the harvest we have loads to eat.
Because it is time to pick our crops.
We have loads of food in England.
We are very *lucky*.
We share food with each other.
When you go to a party you eat a lot,
But when you go home you feel sick and bloated.
You shouldn't waste food,
Because people have to work hard to grow and make it.

Michael Paul (9)
Woodfield Junior School

My Cat

Fizz and me are so alike we're like best friends we never fight.
Her skin is so soft just like mine.
I like to stroke her all the time.
She is never in a bad mood; she's always hungry for her food.
Her tail is so long and soft, it's very sweet like butterscotch.
She's always moving her pointed eyes,
Looking out for tasty flies.
She has white paws and claws for sure.
She's always crying to go outdoors.
In my chair I went and sat, and who jumped up?
My lovely cat!

Kelly-Ann Hegenbarth (9)
Woodgate Primary School

My Day At School

I'm off to school hip, hip, hooray!
Can't wait to see my friends today.
Lots of maths and English too and school dinners.
I hope it's not stew!
It's playtime now, what shall we do?
Gonna play football with you.
Dinner time has gone so quick
Back to class in a tick.
It's PE now and time to play.
I'd love PE every day.
The day has gone oh so quick.
I'll be back home very quick.
Tea and bed, a swim in the pool,
It'll soon be morning - back to school.

Anthony Hegenbarth (7)
Woodgate Primary School

My Friend

My friend is full of care,
My friend has fair hair,
My friend can be mean,
My friend is really keen,
My friend can be quite nice,
My friend has two pet mice,
My friend is the best friend and nothing can top that.

Paige Titley (10)
Woodgate Primary School

The Senses - Oogle Eye

Oogle eye, boogle eye
What can you see?
A river and a mountain
And a tall pine tree.

Oogle eye, boogle eye
What can you hear?
The night and its noises
Ad the sounds of fear.

Oogle eye, boogle eye
What can you smell?
The scent of young flowers
Near the wishing well.

Oogle eye, boogle eye
What can you taste?
Overcooked cabbage
And green fish paste!

Oogle eye, boogle eye
What can you feel?
The cool blue of water
And the silk-skinned seal.

Jarreth-James Copper (9)
Woodgate Primary School

The Seasons

Winter is a time for snow
For rivers to ice and fires to glow

Spring is a time for birdsong
And animals to have their young

Summer is a time for dance
For birds to sing and animals to prance

Autumn is a time for leaves
To blow about and fall off their trees.

Victoria Boucher (9)
Woodgate Primary School

Animal Poem

Seagulls glide
People slide
Birds fly
In the sky
Butterflies flutter
I like butter
Frogs leap
People sleep
Birds eat berries
We eat cherries
Frogs are green
Lions stalk
We walk
Ducks quack
Dogs bark
Horses clop.

Jessica Anderson (8)
Woodgate Primary School

Cat

Taz is the name of my little cat
She plays on our living room mat
She jumps up high -
Thinks she can fly!
She likes to play, play hide-and-seek
She often plays on her own
Because she's all alone.
She has unusual-coloured fur
And she always purrs
She likes to bite
Then she fights
That's my Taz!

Thomas Francis (8)
Woodgate Primary School

Seasons

Winter trees blowing in the breeze
Snow running down the leaves
Snowmen melting to the ground
Oops the sun is coming out
The sun gets covered in clouds
And the snowmen wonder will we live
To June or March or maybe September
Pink blossom growing on the trees
Flowers sprouting, children shouting yippee
Sun shines, bright summer has come
People having water fights
And then the leaves are colourful
Leaves start falling off the trees in autumn
Children jumping in the leaves
Seasons to suit your needs
Adopt your season
Cold seasons, hot seasons which do you like best?

Billy-Jean Copper (10)
Woodgate Primary School

Cats

(Based on 'Cats Sleep Anywhere' by Eleanor Farjeon)

Cats are nice
All they do is sleep
They are loving and cunning
They are furry
They are playful and sleep anywhere
They sleep on the ledge, in the middle, on the edge
And on a lap, and in some cupboard
Cats sleep anywhere.

Peter Saunders (8)
Woodgate Primary School

Where Are You?

Where are you blue kangaroo?
Where are you blue kangaroo?
        I can't see you
Where are you blue kangaroo?
        Where are you?
Where are you orange bear?
Where are you orange bear?
        I can't see you orange bear
        Where are you?
Where are you yellow rabbit?
Where are you yellow rabbit?
        I will give you a carrot
Where are you yellow rabbit?

Rosie Kindon (8)
Woodgate Primary School

Cat

The curious cat
Is very fat
And he barely
Knows what to do
The curious cat
Caught a rat
And he ate
It at dinner
Early.
Then the curious cat
Had a giant hat
Then he gave it to
Old Charlie.

Vincent Binns (8)
Woodgate Primary School

My First Pet

Now I'm eight
I'm allowed something great,
My first pet.

Me and my mum,
Had lots of fun,
We went in and met,
My first pet.

We brought him home,
And made his bed,
Gave him some water,
And made sure he was fed,
My first pet . . .

A hamster.

Connor Murphy (8)
Woodgate Primary School

Cat Kennings

Sly creeper
   Bird eater
Fast runner
   Furry peeker
Spotted tail
   Chicken eater
Lazy cheater
   Nasty sneaker
Purry freaker
   Cats do
      Anything.

Tamika Beckles (8)
Woodgate Primary School

Woodgate School

Woodgate school is fun.
At dinner time we all can run.
We all have lots of friends,
We all write with pens,
At home we have chicks and hens,
God builds houses
God is always kind.
We all have, teachers that are cool,
They are all, good teachers.
We all are good learners,
There is one teacher,
Named Miss Terner.

Jessica Osborn (8)
Woodgate Primary School

My Dog Kennings

A spider killer
A hungry beggar
A fast eater
A door scratcher
A furry friend
A soft sneaker
An ear hearer
A soft growler
An easy waker
A loud barker
A ball catcher
A tail wagger.

Hollie Simmonds (8)
Woodgate Primary School

Fat Rat

Fat Rat
Lived in a hat
He knocked on the door,
Rat-a-tat-tat,
Mighty Mouse
Opened the door
He was fierce and white,
He was strong
Like a knight.
Fat Rat laughed out loud,
But Mighty Mouse
Stood still and proud
Fat Rat laughed himself away,
But he'll be back again one day.

Daisy Duggins (8)
Woodgate Primary School

Dog Kennings

A spider killer
A fast runner
A great jumper
A playful gamer
A tall player
A sharp clawer
A tiger colour
A loving friend.

Keiran Hinde (9)
Woodgate Primary School

Dog

Dogs are mad,
And they are bad,
And so are cats too,
Cats, cats, cats,
Dogs eat meat,
And dogs are mad and bad,
Bugs wiggle,
Dogs jiggle,
And the dog saw
A rat in a hat,
Dogs are fast runners,
And cats are fast too,
Cats are mad,
And dogs are bad.

Abbie Surman (8)
Woodgate Primary School

Dogs

A silent beggar
A food pincher
A spider eater
A fly chaser
A bird killer
A grass eater
A brilliant jumper.

Bradley Penn (8)
Woodgate Primary School

Cat Kennings

Spider killer
Warm sleeper
A bird jumper
A leg climber
A copy cat
Toffee cat
A playful pouncer
A fast dodger
A horrible magnet
Sneeky friend
Tiger sniffer
A lap snatcher
A comfy space pincher
An underwear smeller
A fish lover
A bed roller
A tummy rubber.

Kyle Brunton (8)
Woodgate Primary School